the
answers
to
your
deepest
longings

# contents

# Dear friend,

I remember the day I closed my eyes as tears fell, and I whispered, "God, please either take this longing of my heart away or show me Your answer. I just don't think I can keep hoping for what no longer seems possible."

If you've ever prayed a similar prayer, I want you to know you're not alone. Unmet expectations and longings are tough on the human heart. Especially when what we keep praying for is a good thing ... a reasonable request ... something we see God blessing others with.

And it's at this exact point of desperation that our lives can go in one of two directions. We can press into God and learn to trust Him more fully, or we can give in to the enemy and fall for temptations that will leave us even more empty. If he can get our attention with temptations that falsely promise to ease the ache of an unmet longing, then he can start to fool us with his deceptions. But remember, his ultimate goal isn't to comfort us ... it's to crush us with his accusations.

This is how he works. ***Tempt. Deceive. Accuse.***

He used this method on Eve in the garden. (Genesis 3:6) He tried to use it on Jesus at the end of His 40-day fast in the desert. (Matthew 4:1-11) And it's the same method we are warned about near the end of the Bible in 1 John 2:15-17:

*"Do not love the world or anything in the world. If anyone loves the world, love for the Father is not in them. For everything in the world— the lust of the flesh, the lust of the eyes, and the pride of life—comes not from the Father but from the world. The world and its desires pass away, but whoever does the will of God lives forever"* (NIV).

What does this look like for us today?

## Lust of the flesh

God's not going to provide what I need. I need to take this into my own hands. I need to maintain control.

## Lust of the eyes

God won't give me what I desire. I'm not satisfied with the things God has given me.

## Pride of life/Wanting to appear important

God won't give me what I deserve. I'm going to grasp for it myself.

What our souls are *truly* longing for, though, is more of God. His best is the only source of true satisfaction. He is the only answer to our every desire. He holds all the answers to all our disappointments and will direct our desires in His way, in His will and in His timing. He's got a good plan for good things.

That's why it feels so imperative that we do this study together. For the next 40 days, we'll be feasting on the very thing Jesus used to defeat the enemy at the end of His 40 days of fasting — the Word of God. Eve's dialogue with Satan allowed him to weave his tangled web of justifications. Jesus, on the other hand, shut Satan down with the truth of God.

We don't have to be held hostage by Satan, friend. We are onto him and his schemes. And the enemy's power is nothing compared to the freeing promises of God.

# We're in this together,

*Lysa*

# Leadership

**Lysa TerKeurst**
*President*

**Lisa Allen**
*Executive Director
of Ministry Training*

**Meredith Brock**
*Executive Director
of Strategy and
Business Development*

**Melissa Taylor**
*Senior Director of Online
Bible Studies & First 5*

# Content

**Joel Muddamalle**
*Director of
Theological Reaserch*

**Wendy Blight**
*Online Bible Studies,
Biblical Content Specialist*

**Eric Gagnon**
*First 5 Theological
Content Manager*

**Hannah Schindler**
*First 5 Senior
Project Coordinator*

# Editorial

**Kenisha Bethea**
*First 5 Managing Editor*

**Abbey Espinoza**
*Proofreader/Copy Editor*

# Design

**Riley Moody**
*Senior Manager
of Graphic Design*

# Administrative Support

**Christina Hunter**
*First 5 Coordinator*

# Acknowledgements

The First 5 Team wishes to thank the following for their support of this resource in various ways:

The Proverbs 31 Ministries Executive Team for its leadership, guidance and encouragement: Lysa TerKeurst, Lisa Allen, Meredith Brock, Barb Spencer, Glynnis Whitwer

The Scripture Review Team for double-checking each reference: Ana Brower, Hope Butler, Kelly Catlett, Anita Evans, Kami McKee, Sandra Ann, Sheila Wilson, AdeleAlys Spil, Jackie Bell, Maureen Baugh, Bethany Ruth, Sulette Versteegh

The Focus Group for reviewing the content in its early stages and providing valuable feedback: Quantrilla Ard, Marissa Henley, Stacy Lowe, Nancy Voyles, Katrina Wylie

# Longing

We all long for something or someone. A longing, or a yearning desire, is one of the great shared human realities. Yet, at times we overlook those longings because they're unseen and invisible. It's easy for us to get into a habit of doing, acting, talking and living out of rhythms and routines and overlook that there is something underneath that is driving us. The driving force is longing.

Our longings produce an ache within us, and the enemy loves to use our aches to tempt us to turn away from God and ultimately turn inward to satisfy our longings. Turning inward tempts us to look to things like food, money and success for our satisfaction. But these things, void of God, will leave us restless. James wrote, *"But each person is tempted when he is lured and enticed by his own desire. Then desire when it has conceived gives birth to sin, and sin when it is fully grown brings forth death"* (James 1:14-15).

Scholar, pastor, theologian and church father St. Augustine said, "Our hearts are restless, until they rest in You."[1] Augustine points out a deep truth in the opening pages of Scripture: God created humanity with a longing to love. (Genesis 1-2) There is a spiritual and physical reality to our longing and we see it play out in the human heart.

God designed the human heart to pump blood to our physical body for survival. We need the blood the heart pumps through our bodies in order to work and function the way God intended. In a similar way, the heart spiritually pumps out love. Before the fall, God designed the human heart to pump love and the object of that love was God Himself. God designed us to pump and pour out love from our hearts onto Him. This is worship. However, at the Fall, something went tragically wrong. It's not that the heart ceased pumping love, because we were created with that basic foundational longing to love. Rather, sin damaged our heart, knocking it off kilter, redirecting its love toward objects that promise a sufficient love but only deliver bondage and enslavement instead. Revelation 18:14 describes this damaged longing: *"The fruit for which your soul longed has gone from you, and all your delicacies and your splendors are lost to you, never to be found again!"*

Friends, this kind of longing produces an unending restlessness. We are desperate for satisfaction, yet we are left in an endless cycle of seeking and searching. What's worse is the only thing waiting for us at the end of this longing is loss. However, this does not and should not be our story. The only rest we will find is when our "heart-pumps" realign to the source of true satisfaction that leads to salvation – God Himself. First Peter 2:2 captured this powerfully by saying: *"Like newborn infants, long for the pure spiritual milk, that by it you may grow up into salvation."*

The one true Source to experience this type of satisfaction is found in and through Jesus Christ. Jesus says, *"Do not work for the food that perishes, but for the food that endures to eternal life, which the Son of Man will give to you. For on him God the Father has set his seal"* (John 6:27).

As we journey through the storyline of Scripture in 40 days, we find deeply rooted into the sentences, verses, chapters and books of the Scriptures the reality of longing fleshed out in very specific ways. Humanity essentially longs for eight things that we will discuss each week:

**Week 1** *Purpose*

**Week 2** *Freedom*

**Week 3** *Security*

**Week 4** *Rescue*

**Week 5** *Redemption*

**Week 6** *Fulfillment*

**Week 7** *Identity*

**Week 8** *Christ's Return*

To fulfill our longings, we often look to what my friend Lysa TerKeurst, in her book *It's Not Supposed to be This Way,* refers to as "lesser loves." The pages of Scripture are filled with examples of humanity's feeble attempts to find satisfaction through the pursuit of these eight longings. Longings are not bad in and of themselves, and they are not wrong! However, they can only be truly beneficial when we experience them in and through Christ. As we go through the Bible in 40 days, we will witness both the devastation and great joy of longing.

# Most importantly, we will discover that our longing will find its true rest and satisfaction in Jesus.

# longing for

for ————————— *week one*

# purpose

# Take a moment and recall the first time someone asked you, "What do you want to be when you grow up?"

How old were you? How did you answer that question? Why did you answer the way you did? The answer is directly connected to how we try to find our place in this world. Figuring out our place comes from understanding our purpose. **Purpose.** We long for purpose because God created us for a purpose. Wrapped up in that purpose is the biblical truth that our purpose involves dignity and destiny.

Genesis 1:26-27 reminds us that humanity is made in the likeness and image of God. God graciously bestowed the mark of His image upon His children. This image gives us a status that cannot be taken away and a dignity unlike any other created thing. With this dignity in mind, we are set up to work out God's purpose for our lives. We find the first commission God gave to Adam and Eve in Genesis 1:28, where God gives humanity dominion over the earth and commands them to be fruitful and multiply and fill the earth with image bearers of God. Here we have the foundations of the intended purpose of God for mankind. God intended for His people to be faithful representations of God on the earth and spread His glory from Eden to the ends of the earth. Therefore, humanity's

purpose is intrinsically tied to the work and will of God.

In Genesis 3, the Fall disrupts God's intended purpose for humanity but does not destroy it. We now live in the tension between the purpose of God and the purpose of man. Proverbs 19:21 captures not only the tension but the outcomes: *"Many are the plans in the mind of a man, but it is the purpose of the LORD that will stand."* One of the most important decisions we must make — that is not a one-and-done but a continual intentional decision — is to follow the purpose of God. Sin tempts us to follow our thoughts, intentions and longings for our own purposes, and the fruit of this can tragically result in idolatry.

This week, we will explore the intersection of God's purpose and the purpose of man, beginning with Adam and Eve and wrapping up with Abraham. We will see the great blessing and joy that comes from obedience and submitting to the purpose of God. We will also see the utter destruction that takes place when humanity attempts to exert their own purpose, ignoring and rejecting the purpose of God.

# Creation

### God in His grace created a good world.

*"And God saw everything that he had made, and behold, it was very good..."*
GENESIS 1:31

In the beginning, God created the heavens and the earth. In the beginning, God created everything good. God spoke and transformed formless and empty into light and order. There was no chaos. No evil. Even the darkness of the night had a good purpose to bless and sustain life.

God called His creative work "good" on each day except for the sixth day. On that day, He described his work differently because God created something very special on this day.

*01* | Who does God create? (Genesis 1:27)

*02* | What words did God speak in Genesis 1:26-27? What does it mean to you that you've been made in the image of God?

*03* | **Why do you think God calls His creation "very good" instead of "good"? (Genesis 1:31)**

Genesis 2 gives more specificity on who God created on the sixth day.

*04* | **Read Genesis 2:18 and 21-22. Who else does God create? Circle or write down how many times you see the word "good" in Chapter 2.**

*05* | As we consider the word "longing," what did God identify as lacking in Adam's life? (Genesis 2:18) Who fulfilled that longing? (Genesis 2:21-23) While this is a picture of marriage, it also shows that God has designed humanity for fellowship with one another. Describe a friend or family member for whom you are grateful.

*06* | It's important that we understand "good" to mean more than simply beautiful or well-made. Read Ecclesiastes 7:29. Identify another word that speaks of God's creation and relates to the word "good." What does this teach about how God made mankind?

Tucked in this wonderful, creative work of God, we find a great promise. We find the hope that God has a plan bigger than what we see in the hard places in our lives. Bigger than the mess in which we may find ourselves. These places and messes may frighten, unsettle and confuse us, even lead us to feelings of fear, anxiety and hopelessness. But God. The creation account brings hope. Creation shows us God is an expert at beginnings. Good beginnings. Because of this, we can trust Him when circumstances arise that we may not understand or may question. We can trust Him when He creates or allows circumstances that lead us out of what feels safe and comfortable.

God has not changed since Genesis 1. Scripture tells us He is never-changing. (Malachi 3:6; Hebrews 13:8) The God of Genesis 1 is the God of today and the God of forever. Just as He did during Creation, He is able to bring good to all things. He is able to bring order and beauty in ways that bring hope and confidence.

*07* | One more question to take us a bit deeper. Did you know the Son of God took part in creation? Read John 1:3 and Colossians 1:16 and reflect on what it means to you that God the Son made the world!

# The Fall (Adam and Eve)

Adam and Eve had longings that they tried to fulfill outside of God's design.

---

*"So when the woman saw that the tree was good for food, and that it was a delight to the eyes,*
*and that the tree was to be desired to make one wise, she took of its fruit and ate,*
*and she also gave some to her husband who was with her, and he ate."*

GENESIS 3:6

Chapter 2 ends with Adam and Eve naked without shame. Completely comfortable and vulnerable in who they are with God and with each other. No need to hide anything. No doubt, insecurity, unworthiness, fear, anxiety or regret. They knew their Creator loved them. He surrounded them with peace, pleasure and purpose. Absolute perfection.

Enter the enemy, who spoke four words that stole it all away. *"Did God actually say ... ?"* (Genesis 3:1) Words intended to lure God's children away from their Creator. To separate them from the One in whom they found love and purpose. The One who held their destiny in His hands.

*01*  Name three things Eve longed for that she reasoned the forbidden fruit would fulfill. (Genesis 3:6)

*02*  In what ways do we long for these things today? How might God Himself actually fulfill all of these things in the truest sense? (See for example John 4:34; Proverbs 23:26; Proverbs 2:6)

03 | **Even though Eve ate first, Scripture says Adam "was with her," (Genesis 3:6) and 1 Timothy 2:14 says he "was not deceived." What should Adam have done?**

Satan made into a burden what God spoke as a blessing. Have you heard those lies before? Words intended to deceive you, to turn your heart from the very One who lovingly and intentionally formed and created you and knows you by name? I know I have.

Adam and Eve's choice to believe the enemy over God cut them off from intimate fellowship with God and from God's best gift of all: life forever with Him.

04 | **God told Adam and Eve that if they ate the fruit from the tree of the knowledge of good and evil, they would "surely die" (Genesis 2:17). The serpent said they would not die. (Genesis 3:4) What are two ways in which Adam and Eve died? (Genesis 3:19; Romans 5:12)**

They no longer lived, enjoyed and worked in the safe, beautiful, fruitful garden. God sent them away into a dry, unfruitful land that required sweat and hard work to bear any kind of fruit.

The end of perfection in the Garden of Eden came when Adam and Eve chose to sin. The devil, the liar and father of lies, enticed them away from God's beautiful plan for them. Adam and Eve failed to recognize the work of the enemy.

The good news tucked into this account is that even in the midst of Adam and Eve's bad choices, God is in control. God is greater, stronger and wiser than Satan. God is the Creator; Satan is only a created one. This good news carries forward to God's children today.

**05** | In all of this sin, deception and corruption, we find a glimmer of hope in Genesis 3. What does God say man will do to the serpent? (Genesis 3:15) How is this fulfilled in Romans 16:20?

More good news comes in the New Testament. First John 4:4 gives us a great truth to stand on in our battles, *"Little children, you are from God and have overcome them, for he who is in you is greater than he who is in the world."* Satan and God are not equal. God is all-knowing and all-powerful. Satan is not.

Thankfully, God has made it easier to recognize the enemy at work in our midst. He has given us His written Word that identifies the evil one and outlines his schemes and tactics. This is good news because now we can be on the alert. We know how to recognize him. We won't be caught off guard as Adam and Eve were. Friend, thank God today for the gift of God's Word. Treasure it. Read it. Study it. Pray through it so that the enemy will never have the advantage.

# Noah and the Flood

God flooded the world, but Noah and his family found favor with God.

---

*"But Noah found favor in the eyes of the Lord."*
GENESIS 6:8

Now we meet another of God's created ones. His name is Noah. Noah's godly life stood in stark contrast to the wickedness and evil on display in the lives of the people around him. God's Word tells us *"Noah was a righteous man;" "blameless;"* and that he *"walked with God"* (Genesis 6:9).

01 | Read Genesis 6:5 and write your observations about the thoughts and intentions of mankind's heart during that time.

Noah stood apart. He was different, and his faithful obedience left a mark that will forever sit in the pages of Scripture, etched into God's Story.

We can presume the people mocked Noah as he built this giant boat, explaining that it was because a great flood was coming from the earth and the sky. It probably seemed even more ridiculous because some scholars believe it had never rained on earth before that day. (Genesis 2:4-6; Hebrews 11:7)

It is so much easier to go with the flow. To not rock the boat. To fit in. To follow the crowd.

But, that's not God's way. God commands us to not conform to the pattern of this world. He calls us to be transformed by the renewing of our mind. And we renew our minds through His living and active Word. (Romans 12:2)

Noah did not conform. He allowed His mind to be transformed through God's Word. He heard. He listened. He believed and He obeyed. What about us? What will we choose?

But, Noah was not perfect.

*02* Read Genesis 9:21-25. What happened to show Noah was not perfect? No one is without sin — not even God's best leaders, patriarchs, kings or prophets, (1 John 1:8) and no one does good all of the time. (Ecclesiastes 7:20) Jesus stated that no one is good except God alone. (Mark 10:18) God saw everything and knew everything about Noah, yet what did Noah find in the eyes of the Lord? (Genesis 6:8)

*03* The word "favor" in Genesis 6:8 can also be translated "grace." Write your thoughts here about God's tremendous grace toward Noah and his family. How have you experienced this in your own life?

# The Tower of Babel

## Mankind tried to glorify themselves with a tower but God dispersed them throughout the earth.

---

*Then they said, "Come, let us build ourselves a city and a tower with its top in the heavens, and let us make a name for ourselves, lest we be dispersed over the face of the whole earth."*

GENESIS 11:4

Through these early chapters of Genesis, we see God's people filled with pride and ambition, repeatedly engaging in acts of disobedience. Their prideful ambition led them to fulfill the longing of their hearts in things of the world rather than God. Sound familiar?

This takes us back to the longing discussed at the beginning of this week. We learned that God created us with a longing to be known. However, He intended to fully fulfill that longing with the truth that we are fully known and loved by Him.

*01* | In Genesis 11:4 and 11:8, what did the people fear, and what actually took place?

Like the tower builders, we too often fail to find our fulfillment in God. We seek after the things of this world to satisfy us. Things like recognition, popularity and acceptance by our peers.

In this account, God's people wrongly fulfilled this longing by seeking glory for themselves, not God. Over time, their arrogance led to rebellious acts of defiance that culminated in them uniting to establish a powerful empire for themselves. Rather than looking to God for purpose and destiny, they looked to make a name for themselves.

## curses

02 | Imagine a scenario where they had obeyed God. How do you think this would impact the unity of nations and ethnicities today?

In the Bible, curses often refer to God's holy discipline as a consequence of sin. They began in Genesis when God cursed the ground due to Adam's disobedience. They continued in Deuteronomy when God promised to send blessings or curses, depending upon the people's obedience to His commands. In the New Testament, the Apostle Paul spoke of false teachers saying, *"let him be accursed."* (Galatians 1:8) The Greek word used here is *anathema*, which means to devote to God for judgment.

God's command to His people in Genesis was to *"Be fruitful and multiply and fill the earth"* (Genesis 1:28). Settling in one place and building a tower to the sky directly defied this command. So, God intervened and spoke these words,

*And the LORD said, "Behold, they are one people, and they have all one language, and this is only the beginning of what they will do. And nothing that they propose to do will now be impossible for them. Come, let us go down and there confuse their language, so that they may not understand one another's speech"* (Genesis 11:6-7).

God did just that and scattered them over the face of the earth.

Oh, if only we would know God's commands and His ways are good. Know beyond head knowledge. Know and believe deep in our soul His commands are good. His purposes are good. He is good.

03 | The people building the tower of Babel wanted to make a name for themselves. (Genesis 11:4) They wanted self-glory rather than God's glory. Can you relate? For example, sometimes we work so hard to build our platforms on social media. In and of itself, that's not a bad thing. But, when the motive behind our platform building is not pure, that's when sin enters in. We have to check our hearts. Have there been times when you have desired the attention of others more than God's glory and will in your life?

God calls us to obedience. God blesses and rewards obedience and brings curses and consequences for disobedience. We've watched it with our own eyes in these stories. Whether we understand them or agree with God's commands, we would do well to trust Him and His ways. They are always good, and He is trustworthy.

# Abraham

God promised Abraham would father many nations; he believed and obeyed.

---

*"And he believed the LORD, and he counted it to him as righteousness."*
GENESIS 15:6

God met Abram at a time when he was doubting God's promises. God saw Abram, came to him and spoke great encouragement. *"Fear not, Abram, I am your shield; your reward shall be very great"* (Genesis 15:1). In his old age, Abram focused on the physical: what his eyes could see and what his mind could comprehend. God promised to make him into a great nation, but he had no children. God graciously reassured Abram that a son was coming.

He told Abram to look to the heavens and count the stars and said, *"So shall your offspring be"* (Genesis 15:5).

Without any change of circumstances, Scripture says Abram believed the Lord. He believed God would do what He said He would do. That is faith. And, God responded to Abram's faith by crediting righteousness, right standing with God, as his reward.

## righteousness

Righteousness is an important word for us since it is said that we are counted righteous for believing in Christ. (2 Corinthians 5:21; Romans 4:6-24; 5:19; 10:3) In both Greek and Hebrew, the word is full of meaning. Part of its meaning is doing what is right — that is, obedience to God, and doing justice in the world. The second part of its meaning, and just as important, is the connotation of having a legal right standing before a judge. Both of these meanings are inseparable from each other in the biblical sense of the word.

*01*

As with Noah, righteousness — or right standing with God — did not mean Abram was a sinless person. He simply trusted the Lord. Read Romans 4:4-5. God's Word says this same situation applies to all men and women who trust in the Lord. Describe what it means for you to place your trust in the Lord.

*02* | Reread Romans 4:4-5 and meditate on its meaning, jotting down your thoughts.

God's ways have not changed over these thousands of years. He is the same yesterday, today and forever. Trusting God at His Word ... trusting His promises ... will lead us to righteousness. The key is faith. Abram was renamed "Abraham" by God because of Abram's faith to believe that God would make him the father of many nations. (Genesis 17:5)

*03* | **Faith doesn't mean we never doubt or have questions. In fact, Abraham immediately began asking God how the things He spoke of were possible (Genesis 15:8) and even laughed at other things God promised. (Genesis 17:17) Have you ever doubted God, or asked God why difficult things happen? How were your questions or doubts answered?**

# God's promises are eternal and unchangeable. They will not fail because God cannot fail.

# We can believe the enemy or we can believe God.

We can succumb to lies or stand on Truth. In the garden, Adam and Eve chose to believe the lies of the enemy. Noah and Abram (Abraham), on the other hand, chose to believe the truths of God. Though, let us not forget, Noah and Abraham were not perfect. The times Noah and Abraham failed to follow God and misplaced their longings, God sent harsh consequences as a result.

It seems clear from what we've studied: Choosing lies and self-satisfaction leads to curses and consequences. Choosing truth and humility leads to blessings and fulfillment. Why? Because when we choose to believe lies, we fall into the hands of the enemy. We hear the devil's voice instead of God's, so he determines who we are, our path, even our destiny.

When we trust ourselves, or others, over God, we risk moving so far from God that we forget His heart. His goodness. His love. We forget God's commands are good. His purposes are good. He is good.

Trusting in and obeying God's Word is where we find our true and lasting significance, satisfaction and security.

Abraham lived this well. God had promised to make him into a great nation, yet Abraham found himself without children. How could God's promise come to fruition with no heirs? Was God truly trustworthy?

Abraham cried out to God in discouragement. God came to Abraham and graciously reassured him a son was coming. He reminded Abraham of His promises. Scripture says Abraham believed the Lord ... without any visible proof ... without Sarah being pregnant. Abraham took God at His Word. He believed God would do what He said He would do.

This, my friend, is the essence of faith. God's ways have not changed. God's promises and purposes are eternal and unchangeable. They will not fail because God cannot fail. When the lies of the enemy — fear, doubt, anxiety, unbelief, discouragement — rush in, we must immediately take those thoughts captive. Captive to the Truth of God's Word. The Truth of who we are as children of the One True God.

# Read aloud the truth of who you are in Christ.

## You are Loved.
1 JOHN 3:1

## You are Forgiven.
1 JOHN 1:9

## You are Redeemed.
EPHESIANS 1:7

## You are A New Creation.
2 CORINTHIANS 5:17

## You are Holy.
HEBREWS 10:10

## You are Set Apart.
ROMANS 8:30-39

## You are A Temple of the Holy Spirit.
1 CORINTHIANS 3:16-17; 6:19-20

## You are Made with Purpose.
1 PETER 2:9; 4:10

Now,
pray
and
declare
these
truths
over your
heart and
mind.

# Abba Father, my Creator,

I praise You that I'm fearfully and wonderfully made. Thank You that I am forgiven and redeemed by the blood of Your Son, Jesus. Thank You that in and through the power of Your Holy Spirit, I am a new creation. Because of Your grace and mercy, I am Your hand-crafted masterpiece and You have good and perfect purposes for me. Please grant me wisdom and discernment as I walk out that plan. Help me to discover who You've created me to be. Expose the lies of the enemy. Wash away anything You have not authored for my life. Protect me from the devil's schemes. Give me eyes to see myself, not in the world's eyes, but in Your eyes. Father, may I know deep in my heart that I am holy, created in Your image and set apart for Your purposes. Open my eyes to see my true beauty, a beauty that reflects Your heart, Your character, Your strength and Your dignity. Plant Your Truths deep in my heart. Fill me with Your Holy Spirit and bless me all the days of my life. I ask all this in the name of Your Son, Jesus. Amen.

We realize we can't study every story in the Bible in 40 days. So, along the way, we'll share other important events you can read about on your own.

God called Abraham out of the land of Ur.
**GENESIS 12**

In the first relational dynamic we see between siblings, Cain killed his brother, Abel.
**GENESIS 4**

Mankind tried to glorify themselves with a tower, but God dispersed them throughout the earth.
**GENESIS 11:4**

God in His grace created a good world.
**GENESIS 1:31**

God flooded the world, but Noah and his family found favor with God.
**GENESIS 6:8**

**Job continued to revere God in his suffering.**
JOB 1-3, 38-42

Adam and Eve had longings that they tried to fulfill outside of God's design.
**GENESIS 3:6, 15**

The Lord tested
Abraham's faith
by asking him to
sacrifice his son.
GENESIS 22

Jacob had 12 sons
who became the
tribes of Israel.
GENESIS 29-30

The Lord destroyed
Sodom and Gomorrah
with fire.
GENESIS 19

God promised that Abraham
would father many nations;
Abraham believed and obeyed.
GENESIS 15:6

Isaac had two sons
named Esau and Jacob.
GENESIS 25

Isaac was born, and
Abraham sent his wife
Hagar and Ishmael away.
GENESIS 21

Jacob
wrestled
with God
and was
renamed
"Israel."

GENESIS 35:10

# longing
# for
# freedom

*week two*

# When I was a kid, my dad and I would play a game where he would trap me between his legs, then time me to see how long it took for me to get out. There I was, stuck! Not able to move freely. The weight of his legs holding me down.

Today I do the same thing with my boys. The look on their faces when they finally get out is priceless – freedom! They run, scream, celebrate and usually taunt me all the while!

Prior to the fall, Adam and Eve experienced true authentic freedom. When God said, *"You may surely eat of every tree of the garden, but of the tree of the knowledge of good and evil you shall not eat, for in the day that you eat of it you shall surely die,"* (Genesis 2:16-17) it was the best kind of freedom, because with it came restrictions for Adam and Eve's good. However, after the fall, Adam and Eve traded their true freedom for enslavement and bondage to sin. (Romans 6:20) From that moment on, humanity has been longing for true freedom because we were created and designed to experience freedom. The longing for freedom works itself out in monumental scenes throughout the life of Joseph, who was exiled into slavery by his own brothers and shipped off to Egypt. (Genesis 37:18-36) However, Scripture reminds us that God used Joseph's exile and slavery for good and for the saving of many

lives. (Genesis 50:20) Generations later, Moses, living a lavish lifestyle as a prince of Egypt, exchanged his royal status because he sought freedom for his people, the Israelites, who were under Egyptian captivity. The Israelites themselves would experience liberation through the mighty works of God. However, their story would include a repetitive cycle of freedom, slavery and exile, rescue, and exile again. Every moment the Israelites experienced "freedom," they were actually experiencing a rescue, because they were the covenant people of God and were always intended to live under the perfect and gracious authority of God. (Leviticus 25:42; Deuteronomy 6:20-25)

You may be thinking, *How does this relate to me?* I'm not in captivity, and I haven't experienced exile like the Israelites did. But have you ever experienced feeling stuck in a cycle? You get the job you've always wanted, but then you realize there are parts you really dislike. You may find yourself dissatisfied and start looking for another job. Or, maybe you've worked really hard to eat well and exercise, and you look and feel great! But then, you decide to have a cheat meal that turns into a cheat day that turns into a weekend that turns into weeks. I've done it. Months later, we look in the mirror or at the scale, and we realize we'll have to start all over again. The weight of these circumstances can trap us, leaving us desperate to break the cycle and experience freedom.

It's important to remember that a biblical picture of freedom doesn't mean there are no restrictions. Restrictions aren't God's way of withholding from us; they are God's way of protecting us and often providing something better for us.

# Restrictions aren't God's way of withholding from us; they are God's way of protecting us and often providing something better for us.

Pastor Levi Lusko says, throughout Scripture, wherever we see God saying, *"Don't,"* we should read it as, *"Don't hurt yourself."* True freedom is found when we submit ourselves to the authority of God in Christ Jesus. This truth is seen when God gives the law to His people. The law was never intended to enslave the people of God but to establish a framework that would make known to the surrounding nations that the Israelites were free, yet lived as a people set apart under the authority of Yahweh, the creator God.

As we read and study God's Word together this week, we will come face to face with our own views of what true freedom looks like and challenged to exchange it for God's view. In fact, Joseph, Moses and the Israelites all had their own views of freedom. However, just like them, we will find liberating freedom that will only come when we submit ourselves to the authority and rule of King Jesus. While God delivered the Israelites from the evil grasp of Pharaoh, God in Christ rescued us from the overwhelmingly greater grasp of sin and death. Christ reigned victorious over death and, in doing so, ransomed His people — all those that would repent and submit themselves to the Lordship of Christ — to live in true authentic freedom with Christ the King. (Colossians 2:9-15)

To live in freedom with Christ is to have freedom from the law, because Christ lived to the standard of the law in perfection. To live in freedom with Christ is to have freedom from sin because Christ overcame the power of sin on the cross. And to live in freedom with Christ is to have freedom from death because Christ defeated death, through his death, disarming the evil powers of the world and reigning victorious. [2]

**God saved Moses' life and called him to lead the Israelites.**
EXODUS 3:14

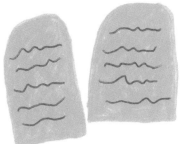

God rescued Joseph from his murderous brothers, and in return, through Joseph, God saved his brothers from famine.
GENESIS 37-50:20

God gave the Ten Commandments.
EXODUS 20:1

God parted the Red Sea and rescued Israel from Egypt.
EXODUS 9:16; 12:50-51

Over time, Israel became enslaved in Egypt and longed for freedom.
EXODUS 1:13

# Joseph

God rescued Joseph from his murderous brothers, and in return,
through Joseph, God saved his brothers from famine.

---

*"As for you, you meant evil against me, but God meant it for good,*
*to bring it about that many people should be kept alive, as they are today."*
GENESIS 50:20

In the closing stories of Genesis, we find a beautiful
account of freedom, forgiveness and mercy.

**01** | **Before we begin, let's sit with the idea of forgiveness for a moment. When it comes to forgiveness, it seems one person always has to give in, even if the other person has not taken responsibility and/or asked for forgiveness. Why do we find it difficult to forgive? What factors do you consider when deciding to forgive someone?**

Now let's study forgiveness in action. In Genesis 42, Jacob sent his sons to Egypt to buy food due to a severe famine in the land. Upon their arrival, Jacob's sons found themselves before their long lost brother, Joseph, who was now governor of Egypt. They did not recognize him, however, because 20 years earlier, Joseph's brothers — driven by jealousy — sold him into slavery.

Despite the dangers, adversities and temptations Joseph encountered while living in Egypt, including years of wrongful imprisonment, he remained faithful to God. It would have been easy for him to be bitter and angry, but there is no record of Joseph complaining. He made an intentional decision to honor God with his words, actions and attitude. The Lord didn't immediately deliver Joseph, but Scripture tells us the Lord remained with Joseph. God protected him during his wrongful imprisonment, freed him from prison, blessed him and eventually elevated him to the second most powerful position in Egypt.

So, when his brothers stood before him, Joseph truly held their fate in his hands. Joseph had a choice before him: He could punish and seek revenge or forgive and seek reconciliation. Joseph chose forgiveness.

02 | Let's look at more Scripture to see how it speaks to forgiveness. Read Matthew 18:21-22. What is Jesus' standard for forgiveness? How do the following passages speak into Jesus' words about forgiveness? (Ephesians 4:32; Colossians 3:13; Matthew 6:12)

Joseph used his position of influence with Pharaoh to bless his father and his brothers. Joseph freed his family from suffering through the famine and settled them in the best part of the land. Without Joseph's favor, his family had no hope of freedom, favor, food, land or provisions.

03 | Are you ready to take a step toward forgiveness? Your heart may not feel like forgiving. But, like Joseph, will you choose to start the process? And, remember, forgiveness does not mean God doesn't value your pain and hurt. They are real. He just doesn't want them to rule your heart and steal the abundant life He has for you on the other side of forgiveness.

We see another beautiful biblical truth played out in Joseph's story. Listen to the powerful words Joseph spoke to his brothers, *"As for you, you meant evil against me, but God meant it for good, to bring it about that many people should be kept alive, as they are today. So do not fear; I will provide for you and your little ones"* (Genesis 50:20-21).

04 | What is the truth Joseph shares with his brothers in Genesis 50:20? Read Romans 8:28 and write it below. How does it speak to what Joseph said to his brothers? What are the two qualifications for this promise to apply?

When the harsh realities of life hit hard, do you still trust God to work in your circumstances to bring you to a place of freedom and favor? Are you willing to trust God enough to patiently wait for the blessings awaiting you on the other side?

05 | **What do you need to trust God with today? Will you trust God at His promise spoken through Joseph, and now to you, that He will work it ALL, every bit of it, for good because you fully belong to Him? You are His beloved child, created with a good plan for a good purpose.**

Joseph's life speaks such hope for us in these times. God is able to transform even the very worst of circumstances for our good and His glory. He is always in control even when it seems our world is out of control.

# Slavery in Egypt

Over time, Israel became enslaved in Egypt and longed for freedom.

---

*"So they ruthlessly made the people of Israel work as slaves."*
EXODUS 1:13

Four hundred years had passed since Joseph moved his family to Egypt. His small family increased in number until they grew to be too numerous to count! (Exodus 1:7; Numbers 1:44-46) These numbers fulfill God's words in Genesis 17:1-8.

*01* | **Read Genesis 17:1-8. List the parts of the covenant God made with Abraham in these verses. Which verse does Joseph's family increase in numbers fulfill? How does Exodus 1:6-7 speak into what we are learning here?**

This increase reveals the absolute faithfulness of our God to honor His Word. What's hard to comprehend is that the fulfillment of this promise led to the enslavement of God's people in Egypt.

But God knew what the Israelites didn't. If they had remained where they had settled before going to Egypt, they would have intermarried, and aligned themselves religiously and politically, with the unbelieving and idolatrous people of that land, including the Canaanites, Moabites and Hittites. The Bible calls these people "pagans." In biblical times, a pagan referred to either those who worshipped many gods or to self-indulgent people who rejected Jehovah as the One True God.

God knew, if left where they were, His holy, set-apart people would have absorbed into the pagan culture, forgetting who and whose they were.

No matter what happened in Egypt, God's good and perfect plan would stand. The plan that God would eventually bring His people into Canaan, the land God promised Abraham. Not even the wickedness and cruelty the Egyptians inflicted upon the Israelites could thwart the plan God set forth before time began. It could not nullify the promises made to Abraham, Isaac and Jacob.

It's hard to understand how enslavement ... this depth of cruelty and suffering ... could be allowed by God to accomplish His plan for His people. Yet, it was.

Have you ever asked, "Why has God allowed this?" "God, how could this be Your plan?" I know I have. If we want to walk closely with God, we must keep our minds fixed on one significant character trait of our God. His Sovereignty.

02 | **What does "sovereign" mean when it comes to God? It means He has all power and authority in this world. Look up these verses and share what you learn: Psalm 24:1-2; 47:7; Matthew 28:18; John 1:3. John Piper summarizes God's sovereignty like this: God's sovereignty is His right and power to do all that He decides to do.**

So, though our circumstances sometimes make no sense, if these verses are true, and God controls all things, including our stories, then there are no accidents.

03 | **Read Acts 17:25-26 and Psalm 139 for more insight into God's involvement in and over our lives.**

God's sovereignty is not limited to the Old Testament. God's sovereignty is part of who He is. So is love. God is sovereign, and God is love. His sovereignty is wrapped in His love. So much love that God willingly surrendered His one and only Son to reveal that love. God suffered and grieved, executing His own plan of redemption, as He watched the soldiers lay His Beloved Son on the cross and hammer the nails in one by one.

God sent His one and only Son Jesus to free us, just as He freed the Israelites. He freed us from the slavery of sin and death we are born into because of Adam and Eve's choices in Genesis 3. The way to freedom is believing in Jesus. The way to freedom is to confess our sin, and turn to Jesus to forgive that sin and bring us into an everlasting loving relationship with God the Father, God the Son and God the Holy Spirit.

Oh, friend, tuck this image of the cross, and these words from Paul, deep within your heart for those times you ask, "God, how could this be your plan?" Remember what God did in Christ Jesus He did for you. Trust may not come in the moment. But, it will settle into your heart as you come to know and trust God's love and character more deeply. God has good plans for us, just as He did for Noah, Abraham, Moses and Israel.

# Moses and the Burning Bush

God saved Moses' life and called him to lead the Israelites.

---

*God said to Moses, "I AM WHO I AM." And he said, "Say this to the people of Israel: 'I AM has sent me to you.'"*
EXODUS 3:14

As Exodus 3 opens, we find Moses in a most extraordinary encounter,
standing next to a burning bush wrestling through his doubts with God.

*01* | **Where else do we see God revealing Himself, or His will, accompanied by fire? See Exodus 13:21, 15:7, 19:18 and Malachi 3:2-3. What does Hebrews 12:29 say about God?**

Why would God choose fire? Because throughout Scripture, God presents fire as purifying and refining. It separates the impurities and leaves what is valuable. Friend, when God brings or allows the fiery furnace of discomfort in our lives, it does not burn indiscriminately. It burns intentionally, to make us more like Him. We can trust that it is always for our refinement and never for our destruction. God knew Moses was about to walk with God's people through some serious refining.

God knew Moses lacked what He needed to step into His assignment. So, the fire was dramatic. Necessary. A powerful reminder of who God was, who Moses was and who God was calling him to be.

In Exodus 3:11, Moses, who had been hiding as a fugitive for 40 years, questioned God's assignment.

Moses asked, *"Who am I that I should go ... and bring the children of Israel out of Egypt?"*

God simply replied, *"I will be with you"* (Exodus 3:12).

It is interesting that God doesn't build up Moses' confidence. He simply gives Moses a promise. He affirmed that He would be with Moses.

Moses asks for more assurance. Who exactly is it that will be with him as he returns to Egypt?

God then gives Moses a special revelation of who He is. God gives Moses a new name to call Him. God says, *"I AM WHO I AM"* (Exodus 3:14). Though the meaning of this name is not completely certain, one possible meaning is "I will be to you All that I AM."

How I love this name God has given Moses in the midst of the fear of the unknown! God knew what lay ahead for Moses. Moses did not. Through this name, God promised to be EVERYTHING Moses needed. Everything Israel needed to ensure the nations around them knew that the Israelite's God was the One True God.

*02* | **How do the following New Testament passages undergird what we have learned in today's reading? (Romans 8:35-37, 1 Peter 1:6-7 and James 1:2-4)**

What a beautiful reminder that who we are is not nearly as important as who God is.

Again, as we did last week, we need to ask where, or to whom do we look to fill our longings? More specifically, to pause and ask, in whom do we place our faith? In the things of this world? In idols, as the pagan nations did? In making a name for ourselves, like the ones who built the tower of Babel? Or do we place our faith in the God of Abraham, Isaac and Jacob? In Israel's God? The One True God?

Friend, God, who is our great "I Am," fulfills every longing of our hearts. Jesus carries this truth forward into the New Testament as He declares His many magnificent names. He is the Bread of Life sent so we never need to hunger or thirst again. (John 6:35) He is the Light of the World so we never have to walk in darkness again. (John 8:12) He is the Good Shepherd who will lead us so we never feel anxious, fearful, lost or alone again. (John 10:11) He is the Resurrection and the Life who guarantees abundant life here on earth and forever in Heaven with Him. (John 11:25)

Take a few moments to ponder where you place your faith when you doubt, fear the unknown or question God's actions. Is your faith based on you or is it anchored in who God is? His character. His Word. His power. His very presence living within you.

# "I am."

## "I am the bread of life."
### (JOHN 6:35,41,48,51)
*As bread sustains physical life, so Christ offers and sustains spiritual life.*

## "I am the light of the world."
### (JOHN 8:12)
*To a world lost in darkness, Christ offers Himself as a guide.*

## "I am the door of the sheep."
### (JOHN 10:7,9)
*Jesus protects His followers as shepherds protect their flocks from predators.*

## "I am the resurrection and the life."
### (JOHN 11:25)
*Death is not the final word for those in Christ.*

## "I am the good shepherd."
### (JOHN 10:11,14)
*Jesus is committed to caring and watching over those who are His.*

## "I am the way, the truth, and the life."
### (JOHN 14:6)
*Jesus is the source of all truth and knowledge about God.*

## "I am the true vine."
### (JOHN 15:1,5)
*By attaching ourselves to Christ, we enable His life to flow in and through us.*
*Then we cannot help but bear fruit that will honor the Father.*

# Rescue from Egypt

God parted the Red Sea and rescued Israel from Egypt.

---

*"But for this purpose I have raised you up, to show you my power,*
*so that my name may be proclaimed in all the earth."*

EXODUS 9:16

As we meet Moses in the midst of the plagues God brought upon Egypt, he has grown and matured. Moses no longer doubted, questioned or complained. We see no fear or hesitation. Whatever God commanded Moses to do, He did it. Immediately.

The time had arrived for Moses to step up and do what God called him to do that day at the burning bush. To free God's people and lead them out of Egypt. (Exodus 3:10) Through Moses and the mighty works of God, the Israelites would finally experience freedom and liberation.

01 | **What do you think caused this transformation in Moses? What can we learn from the following Scriptures to help us trust God more when He calls us to do a hard thing? (Deuteronomy 31:6, Psalm 27:1, Hebrews 10:36 and James 1:12)**

Through the sending of plagues, God ensured Pharaoh knew that He was in control. Each plague offered an opportunity for Pharaoh, and Egypt, to repent and acknowledge Israel's God as the One True God, and to understand and fear God's sovereignty, His might and power. God made it very clear: The more resistance Pharaoh gave, the more plagues God would bring. And with every act of resistance on Pharaoh's part, the more glory and attention fell on the majesty and power of Israel's God. Pharaoh's stubborn refusal opened the way for God to reveal His power and declare His name throughout the earth the way He did.

We see this happen again in the New Testament with the Jewish rulers who crucified Jesus. God didn't plant jealousy and hatred in their hearts. He simply gave them up to their own evil and selfish inclinations (Romans 1:24-28) so that He again could accomplish His Kingdom purposes laid out before time began.

Let's revisit our longings for a moment. Pharaoh and the Jewish rulers sought to satisfy the bent of their fallen human hearts (their longings) through power and control. Yet another example of misplaced desires. Their choices clearly reveal the consequences of living outside of God's will and plan for our lives.

How thankful I am we have Jesus. As children of God, we are different. We have Jesus. Because of Jesus, the One who created us now lives within us. His Spirit in us brings us deep soul satisfaction that cannot be found in more power, more control, more recognition. When we follow the longings of God's heart, and not our own, God blesses us with a satisfied, abundant and full life.

*02* | **Looking back to the Fall in Genesis 3, God gives us a clear picture of two truths. First, God has all authority over Creation and His created ones. Second, despite His children's rebellious acts, God continues to desire relationships with them. He continues to work to redeem them from their fallen state. How are these two truths played out in the biblical account of Moses? How does God's desire for redemption, and His compassion for His children, play out through the pages of Scripture? Choose one or two examples.**

In the end, God will have His way in the lives of His children. The question is, will we willingly join Him in His work, like Moses did, and experience His freedom and partake in the glorious results? Or, will we fight and resist and be a mere tool in His hands like Pharaoh?

The stories we've studied reveal that, without God's intervention, God's created ones follow the bent of their own fallen hearts. That fact does not change as we journey into the New Testament. We still encounter fallen people. We are fallen people. But, for those who are children of God, our hearts are different. The blood of Jesus has freed us, cleansed us, renewed us and infused us with God's deep and abiding love. The One who created us now lives within us. Leading, speaking, convicting and guiding.

*03* | **Reading that last paragraph and the following Scriptures, why is God's plan to redeem humanity the only plan that has the power to work; the only plan that truly brings freedom? (Acts 13:38-39, Romans 6:22, Romans 8:1-4; Galatians 5:22-26)**

# The Ten Commandments

### God gave the Ten Commandments.

---

*"And God spoke all these words ..."*

EXODUS 20:1

The people had arrived at Mt. Sinai. God told Moses to prepare and consecrate the people because in three days He would come down on the mountain to speak to them. By the third day, over two million people anxiously awaited the arrival of Yahweh, the One True God.

A thick cloud swallowed the mountain. It trembled violently and smoke appeared as the voice of God spoke, *"all these words"* (Exodus 20:1).

*What words did God speak?*

## He spoke the Ten Commandments.

God's moral law, setting a new and holy standard for His people to live by. Remember, God created us with longings. He knew circumstances would arise that would lead His people astray into misplaced longings and affections. So, He set down these commands to steer His children's hearts back to Him.

When I've read this passage over the years, I usually jump right into the Ten Commandments. But, as I prepared for this teaching, I read the introductory words. I've never paid attention to them before, but they are powerful. Just before God set forth His Ten Commandments, He spoke these words:

*"I am the Lord your God who brought you out of Egypt, out of the land of slavery"* (Exodus 20:2).

Friend, it's from these beautiful, grace-filled words that the other commandments flow. God sent the Ten Commandments to bring freedom! God didn't rescue His people from slavery to subject them to it all over again through His law. Our gracious and loving God sent His commands not to restrict and burden, but to free His people to love more deeply and live an abundant and full life in Him.

# What are these commands?
(See Exodus 20:1-17)

## The first four are vertical commands
*(They address our relationship with God):*

1

2

3

4

## The last six are horizontal
*(They address our relationships with other people):*

5

6

7

8

9

10

God not only spoke these words, He wrote them on stone tablets for His people to have and to treasure. But as with everything we've studied so far, everything in the New Testament gets better! With Jesus' death and resurrection, words that were once only etched in stone are now etched into the heart of every child of God. Into your heart and mine! Living, active, penetrating words put there to not only teach us but to save, heal, bless, encourage, equip, protect and guide us.

*01* | **Read Jeremiah 31:31-34. What is Jeremiah saying will happen in the future? Read Hebrews 8:6-13. What does the author of Hebrews say here?**

Jeremiah gives God's people a prophetic declaration that a new and different covenant was coming. This new covenant, ushered in by Jesus, enables God's children — you and me — to internalize God's law, love the law and seek to obey it willingly. The new covenant does not change the moral law set forth in the Ten Commandments. They are universal and eternal standards of righteousness for the people of God. But now, rather than written on stone, they are written in our hearts to redirect us back to God's very best for us. And, because of the gifts of God's deep and abiding love, and His Holy Spirit indwelling us, we have a new heart and new spirit that fully equips us to walk out every command in love and with love.

**Read John 14:15, 21 and John 15:9-11.**

*02* | **The question for us to meditate on as we close today is this: Do we value God's Word? His God-breathed Word. Do we not just ingest it, but also digest it? Do we spend time in it and hide it in our hearts? Do we allow it to form and shape us from the inside out so we can walk in the fullness of God's precious new covenant love given to us by Jesus?**

# Joseph's life is a beautiful story of freedom, redemption and forgiveness.

When Joseph's brothers came before him in Egypt, he had a choice to make: Would he seek revenge or reconciliation? Joseph chose forgiveness and blessing, settling his family in the best part of the land.

The Israelites multiplied greatly in Egypt before their slavery and continued despite their slavery. We came to understand from our study that if God's people had remained where they had settled, they would have fully assimilated into the pagan culture.

Sitting in the consequences of our disobedience and rebellion is painful. But, as this week's readings show, God is always working, even in our hard spaces and places. Working for our good, and for His sovereign will to be accomplished.

God raised up Moses to free His people from slavery. In Moses' wrestling with God about this call to lead His people, God gave Moses a new name to describe Himself: I AM WHO I AM. With this revelation, Moses' faith and confidence increased. He shifted his eyes off of what he felt he couldn't do and onto what he knew God could do. Oh, friend. What a beautiful reminder that who we are is not nearly as important as who He is. Moses' faith allowed him to persevere through every plague.

Once free, the people encountered the power and presence of the Great I AM in a most spectacular way as He gave them the law. Before speaking the individual Ten Commandments, God spoke beautiful, grace-filled words from which all the commandments flow. Words of freedom!

God sent the law to bring freedom! Our gracious and loving God sent His law not to restrict and burden, but to free His people to live an abundant and full life in Him.

God's words didn't remain etched in stone. With Jesus' death and resurrection, by the power of the Holy Spirit, God etched His words into the heart of every child of God. Not to burden and enslave us but to free us!

When asked by a scribe — a modern day term for lawyer — which of the 10 commandments was greatest, Jesus, instead of promoting one law over another, defines the essence of God's law. He spoke these words,

*And he said to him, "You shall love the Lord your God with all your heart and with all your soul and with all your mind. This is the great and first commandment. And a second is like it: You shall love your neighbor as yourself"* (Matthew 22:37-39).

Jesus drilled down to the core of the law. The heart behind the law: Love. He narrowed them down to two. The vertical love for God. And, the horizontal love for others. Love God with everything you are and have and love your neighbor as yourself. When we love God like this, obedience will follow and an abundance of fruit will flow. His love will manifest itself in ways we never dreamed possible.

# Father, thank You that You have delivered me

from the power of darkness into the Kingdom of Light. You have set me free from the law of sin and death. You say I'm no longer a slave but your child. So, today, I choose to live in that freedom. I choose to not align myself with this world. I choose to not sink into darkness but to walk confidently in the Light. I cast all my insecurities, anxieties, worries and fears on You, The Great I Am. I choose to fix my mind on what is true, honest, just, pure and worthy of praise — Your Word, Your love, Your hope. I ask all this in Jesus' name. Amen.

A year of rest was
prescribed by God,
which is a symbol of
the coming eternal
rest and joy in Christ.
**LEVITICUS 25-26**

# Instructions
# on
# offerings
# were
# given.
**LEVITICUS 1**

Instructions for the
Day of Atonement
were given, a notable
symbol of Jesus'
future work.
**LEVITICUS 16**

The Israelites grumbled
to God about their
food preferences and
were disciplined.
**NUMBERS 11**

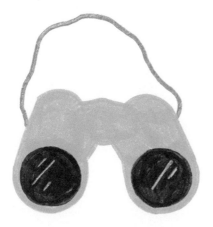

The Ten Commandments were repeated again to the new generation.
DEUTERONOMY 5-6

The promised land was spied out, and only Joshua and Caleb gave a hopeful report, further delaying entry to the land.
NUMBERS 13-14

As a symbol of Christ's future work on the cross, a pole with a bronze snake was set up to save those who beheld it.
(NUMBERS 21:4-9)
(ALSO SEE JOHN 3:14-15.)

God Himself wrote the Ten Commandments again on new tablets of stone.
DEUTERONOMY 10:4

# longing for

## for ———————— *week three*

## security

# Take a moment and consider what makes you feel safe.

For some of us, it's a particular person or people like our family. For others, it's the comfort and familiarity of home. Still, for others, it's access to tangible resources or objects that provide a sense of stability in what can often feel like a very unstable world. What we are ultimately describing is a sense of security. The Israelites held to God's promise that He would give them a land flowing with *"milk and honey"* (Exodus 3:17). The Israelites saw the nations around them with lands, cities, resources and places of worship, and yet after their captivity in Egypt, they spent much of their time wandering and waiting to arrive at the promised land.

As we follow the story of the Israelites, we discover that their journey to the promised land was as important, if not more important, than their actual arrival in the promised land. Why? Because along the way, the Israelites learned how to trust. They had to trust in God's direction, protection and provision. Interestingly, the Old Testament has roughly 19 different Hebrew terms for "secure," "securely" and "security." The most commonly used is the Hebrew word *bā·ṭaḥ,* which refers to a reliance or confidence placed in a person or object. (2 Kings 18:5) [3] God used the Israelites' journey as an opportunity for them to learn to trust in Him as their God who provided for and protected them. This was an important lesson to learn before they experienced the abundance in the promised land. Afterward, it would have been easy for them to shift their trust from God as their source of security to cities, walls, armies and kingdoms.

King David reminds us that God provides security to those who seek refuge in Him:

*"For who is God, but the LORD? And who is a rock, except our God? This God is my strong refuge and has made my way blameless. He made my feet like the feet of a deer and set me secure on the heights"* (2 Samuel 22:32-34).

As we walk through this week's scriptures, let's begin by considering our own individual journeys. In who or what do we find our security? What happens when those things fail us? Theologian and preacher Charles Spurgeon once gave an illustration where a man locked all of his precious belongings in a safe and then bolted the door to the room the safe was in, thinking it would provide him with security. In the middle of the night, he heard a sound and ran to see if a thief had come and stolen his treasure. He unlocked the bolt to the room and opened the safe to find his treasure safe and sound. He then locked everything up and returned to his bed only to hear another noise and wonder again if it was a thief. This happened night after sleepless night. What he thought would bring security did not. Spurgeon contrasted this illustration with the security the Christian finds in Christ, "The safety of the Christian's treasure is of quite another sort. His soul [is] not under bolt and bar, or under lock and key of his own securing, but he has transferred his all to the King eternal, immortal, invisible, the only wise God, our Saviour—and such is his security that he enjoys the sleep of the beloved, calmly resting, for all is well." [4]

What if the journey or wilderness that we're experiencing right now is God's invitation to put our reliance and confidence in Him? If we view our experience through this lens, we may gain a security that enables us to sleep soundly through the night because it's grounded in the knowledge that God is in control and nothing can fall out of His grasp, therefore all is well.

**By faith, a gentile named Rahab helped the Israelite spies.**

JOSHUA 2

God gave the Israelites the city of Jericho.

JOSHUA 5-6

Longing for security, but ignoring the warnings of Deuteronomy 20:16-20, most but not all Canaanite kings were defeated by Israel.

JOSHUA 12

The land of Canaan was again promised to Joshua as an inheritance.

JOSHUA 1:6

God stopped the waters of the Jordan River, allowing the Israelites to cross into Canaan.

JOSHUA 3

The land was divided among Israel's tribes.

JOSHUA 13-21

# The Promised Land

The land of Canaan was again promised to Joshua as an inheritance.

---

*"Be strong and courageous, for you shall cause this people to inherit the land that I swore to their fathers to give them."*
JOSHUA 1:6

Sometimes God calls us to assignments that seem far beyond our gifts and abilities. I wonder if that's how Joshua felt when God called him to receive the promised inheritance and settle in Canaan, the Promised Land.

*01* | **Read Deuteronomy 12:10. What did God promise to give His people once they entered into their promised inheritance?**

The Israelites had no idea how significant and precious those promises of rest and safety would be in the coming years. Remember, God's people lived enslaved in Egypt for hundreds of years, so Egypt represented slavery and bondage.

God's requirement for Israel to receive her inheritance, and the Canaan rest that accompanied it, was to trust in God and His promises. Sadly, that first generation of Israelites never received their promised inheritance because they failed to fully trust God, so God kept them from enjoying the rest and fruitful abundance awaiting them in the Promised Land.

But God! The time had come for Joshua to usher the second generation of God's people across the border into their blessed inheritance. To walk in, and fully enjoy, Canaan rest — the blessings of freedom and rest from all their enemies.

*02* | **Read Joshua 3:9-17. What happened in this story? What was the miracle?**

What a glorious day!! The people received what God had promised hundreds of years before it came to be.

Do you want even more good news? God's promised rest did not end in Canaan. It did not end with the Israelites. We too have a promised rest. One that is bigger and better because of Jesus.

The author of Hebrews writes, *"... the promise of entering his [God's] rest still stands ..."* (Hebrews 4:1).

Friend, this day reveals another longing God knew His people would need fulfilled. The longing for peace and security and for our souls to be at rest. The physical rest promised to Israel in the Promised Land is a picture of the spiritual rest we find in Jesus when we give our lives to Him. Jesus gives us the peace *"which surpasses all understanding"* (Philippians 4:7). This peace is from a source not found on this side of heaven. It is the heavenly fruit of God's Spirit who comes to live in us when we invite Jesus to be our Lord and Savior. (Galatians 5:22)

How does it work? Like the Israelites, we too were slaves. Slaves to sin and death. It's only when we recognize our sin, confess our sin and give our lives to Christ that we can enter into Jesus' promised rest and receive His unsurpassing peace.

The author of Hebrews issues a warning to God's people regarding this promise of rest. He writes, *"let us be careful that none of you be found to fall short of it"* (Hebrews 4:1, NIV).

Friend, just like our Israelite brothers and sisters, we must fully trust God and His promises to enter into our rest. Take notice of the miracles that happen if we do: First, when we surrender our heart, mind and body to Jesus, God gives us right standing with Him through the blood of His Son, Jesus. This forgiveness, this freedom from sin and death, gives us peace with God. This is that salvation rest ... peace with God.

Second, in that moment of salvation, God seals us with His Spirit. This means the Spirit of the Living God comes to live in us. And, with His Spirit, we receive the fruit of His Spirit. This is the peace of God.

*03* | Read Galatians 5:22-23. List the fruit of the Spirit.

Did you notice that one evidence of the fruit of the Spirit is peace? This makes salvation a two-fold gift: We receive peace with God and the peace of God. The peace of God is the peace that passes all understanding. The peace that guards our heart and mind. The peace that the world cannot give. The peace that is our promised rest.

*04* | Read Matthew 11:28-30. What does it say about rest? What does this passage speak to your heart?

As children of God, we have the comfort of knowing we have salvation rest — peace with God. Rest that guarantees we get to spend eternity with Jesus. But, we also have peace for today — the peace of God. Let's not miss living confidently in the peaceful, fruitful, abundant life made available to us in Jesus.

# What keeps you from experiencing God's rest today?

# Abba Father, Your Word promises

that whoever believes in You will have streams of living water flowing from her heart. From that living water flows peace and rest. We have given our hearts to You. We are Your blood-bought children. Our names are engraved in the palm of Your hand for all eternity.

Father, we are thirsty. We long for that living water to flow in all its fullness through us today and every day. Fill us afresh right now. Fill us to overflowing with the peace, rest, hope and joy that is ours in You simply because You call us Your children.

Lead us beside still waters. Restore our weary souls. Sustain us in these difficult times. Let us REST and TAKE REFUGE in You and You alone. Keep us SECURE under the shadow of Your wings.

Help us know that You are near. Give us ears to hear Your gentle whispers. Settle our souls amidst the stress and strain of what each day holds. Enable our settled souls to take captive our scattered minds and center them on Truth and Truth alone.

And Jesus, who is the King of kings and Lord of lords, remind us of what's to come. The day we will receive the crown of life. The day we will forever eat from the tree of life. The day we will physically be in Paradise with You and our Abba Father … in Your presence … worshipping, reigning and ruling with You in glory. (2 Timothy 2:11-13)

We love you, Lord, and ask all this in Jesus' most precious and glorious name. Amen.

It's so hard to walk in the fullness of this peace, but it is ours in Christ! So, let peace settle into your soul and when fear, worry and anxiety rear their ugly heads, let your settled soul boss your scattered mind around. Tell the devil you won't accept his lies. Tell him Jesus died for you so you could walk fully in your promised inheritance and walk securely in the peace that surpasses all understanding. Fully in the One who is your Prince of Peace.

# Judges

The Lord provided Israel with judges to satisfy their longing for security from their enemies, but Israel did not listen to their judges.

---

*"Whenever the LORD raised up judges for them, the LORD was with the judge, and he saved them from the hand of their enemies all the days of the judge. For the LORD was moved to pity by their groaning because of those who afflicted and oppressed them. But whenever the judge died, they turned back and were more corrupt than their fathers, going after other gods, serving them and bowing down to them. They did not drop any of their practices or their stubborn ways."*

JUDGES 2:18-19

Sin. God's people struggled then, and we struggle now, with the problem of sin. Whether we ignore it, hide it or flaunt it, eventually we'll have to confront it. This truth unfolds before our eyes in the book of Judges. Joshua died and a new generation arose who had not witnessed firsthand the miracles and provision of God. Throughout Judges, we watch this next generation of God's people sin. That sin follows a dangerous cycle. First, they abhorred sin. Then they endured it. Then, they tolerated it. And finally, they embraced it. Sin has a vicious appetite. (James 1:13-16) The people's desire for what God restricted escalated into defiance and rebellion that resulted in devastating consequences.

This pattern has not changed. We succumb to sin and temptation today. We prefer to blame Satan for our sinful choices. And, yes, Satan tempts us. But, the only reason his temptings succeed is because of our own fallen nature. A nature that corrupts our God-given desires and draws us away from the good things of God — the security, peace, goodness and hope found only in Him.

Sixteenth-century theologian John Calvin said it well, "Scripture asserts that the reprobate are delivered up to depraved lusts; but is it because the Lord depraves or corrupts their hearts? By no means; for their hearts are subjected to depraved lusts, because they are already corrupt and vicious." [5]

As we read these stories, it's hard to watch God remain faithful to His people and watch as His faithfulness is rarely reciprocated. Instead, God's people continually did evil in the eyes of the Lord. Their unfaithfulness led to harsh consequences.

Judges 2 provides a glimpse into these consequences.

01 | Read Judges 2:1-4, 16-23. What did the angel of the Lord remind God's people? How did the people disobey? What were the consequences?

02 | Where do you find yourself in the cycle of sin — abhor, endure, tolerate, embrace? Is there an area of sin you know God wants you to deal with, but you continue to ignore?

The stories in Judges teach that disobedience will lead to hard consequences. God's standards don't change with time. We too will face consequences when we disobey God's commands and fail to trust Him at His Word. In Judges 2, God removed His presence and protection from His people.

But God! He never forgets His children. God again declared His commitment to keep the covenant He made with Abraham, Isaac and Jacob. There would be consequences, yes, but God would remain faithful to His Word.

03 | God is Judge, but He is also our covenant-keeping God. What does it mean to you when you read God's words, *"I will never break my covenant with you"*? (Judges 2:1)

Satan strategizes day and night to steal our eternal security found only in Christ. He wants to convince us that giving into and pursuing our corrupt desires will bring the security we desperately desire and produce the good and abundance we lust after. That is such a lie! When confronted with Satan's lies, let's remember these words from Jesus in the book of John,

# The thief comes only to steal and kill and destroy. I came that they may have life and have it abundantly.

## JOHN 10:10

Let these words soak into your heart as you consider your answer to the cycle of sin question above. Sit with God today. Lay your sin before Him. Pray and ask for forgiveness and for the strength to turn away from the sin and back toward Jesus.

Friend, there's a formula for freedom from the bondage of sin. It requires that we recognize our sin, repent of it, turn from it and change our behavior. My prayer for us today is that we humbly place our longings and desires in the hands of our loving, grace-filled God and invite Him to transform our hearts and align them with His. Then may we eagerly await the secure, rich and abundant life He has for us on the other side of the journey.

# Kings

The Israelites asked God for a king, which God said is a rejection of Him.

---

*"And in that day you will cry out because of your king, whom you have chosen for yourselves, but the LORD will not answer you in that day."*

1 SAMUEL 8:18

In 1 Samuel 8, the elders demanded that God's prophet, Samuel, give them a king. Israel had no kings because God was their King. But, as their population grew, the Israelites longed for a king like they saw in the unbelieving nations surrounding them (the nations who did not worship the One True God). They thought this earthly king would bring the security, power, recognition and respect they so desperately wanted.

Samuel, angry and displeased with their request, prayed to God. The Lord comforted Samuel with these words: *"... it is not you they have rejected, but they have rejected me as their king. As they have done from the day I brought them up out of Egypt until this day, forsaking me and serving other gods, so they are now doing to you"* (1 Samuel 8:7-8, NIV).

God told Samuel to warn them of the terrible acts the king for whom they were asking would commit against them. Samuel told them in 1 Samuel 8:10-18 that this king would demand much of them and take everything they held precious. What the Israelites didn't know is God intended they would one day have a king, a good king, but God wanted to appoint that king in His timing and His way.

*01* | **How did the people respond to Samuel's warning? (1 Samuel 8:19-20)**

*02*    **What did God tell Samuel to do? (1 Samuel 8:22)**

*03*    **The people's rejection of God as their King is quite prophetic. Read John 19:1-16 and explain what is happening here. Who was rejected as King?**

*04*    **What does Scripture tell us about this King? (Matthew 28:18; Philippians 2:5-11; Hebrews 1:1-4)**

God had a better plan. God knew a better King was coming. One who would fulfill their every longing and desire. One who would satisfy their every need. One who would provide for their every need. God knew the One whose name is King of kings and Lord of lords was coming. (Revelation 19:16) This literary structure, "King of kings" and "Lord of lords" means more than the establishment of a position of kingship. This structure indicates the Second Coming of Jesus and the supremacy of Jesus as the One and Only King. A King in the highest possible sense of Kingship. Jesus not only reigns now, but He alone will reign and rule as the King and Lord of all the earth for all eternity! (Acts 1:10-11)

# Saul

## God raised up Saul to be king, and he failed to seek God.

---

*"Tomorrow about this time I will send to you a man from the land of Benjamin, and you shall anoint him to be prince over my people Israel. He shall save my people from the hand of the Philistines. For I have seen my people, because their cry has come to me."*

### 1 SAMUEL 9:16

Even though Israel had rejected God as their king. Even though they failed to trust in God's direction, protection and provision. God remained in control. He still held them secure in the palm of His hand. God didn't hand over His eternal Kingship just because the Israelites rejected Him. (1 Samuel 8:7) Instead, He gave them the earthly king they demanded. A flawed king. The kind of king about which Samuel warned against.

Samuel introduced their first king, Saul, in 1 Samuel 9:1-2, describing him as *"a man of wealth,"* and *"not a man among the people of Israel more handsome than he. From his shoulders upward he was taller than any of the people."*

God's people admired Saul, not for his character, but for his outward appearance and standing. Saul fit the bill for their flesh-driven desire to have a king that looked like their pagan neighbors they so desperately longed to be like. Again, God's people were looking for their security not in God but in the things of this world — outward appearance, power and prestige.

God confirmed Saul's assignment as Israel's first king with an anointing, three signs and the infilling of the Holy Spirit. Saul's anointing was an outward symbol of what was being done inwardly.

## Let's take a few minutes to study anointing and anointing oil.

*01* | Read Exodus 30:22-33. What do you learn about anointing oil?

Oil was used in the Old Testament to set priests, prophets and kings apart for service to God. After God anointed Saul, God then poured out His Spirit on Saul to set him apart for his assignment to be the very first king of Israel.

*02*     **Who else received God's Spirit at the start of His ministry? Read Luke 3:21-23.**

*03*     **Who else receives God's Spirit? (John 14:15-18, 25-26; Ephesians 1:13-14)**

Hallelujah! Thank You, Jesus, for giving us Your Spirit of Truth to fill, encourage, lead, guide and teach us.

Initially, it seemed God's crowning of Saul humbled him. Saul experienced success, and God blessed his humility and obedience.

Saul's humility didn't last long. He soon began to take matters into his own hands. On one occasion, insecure with God's role in his kingship, fear and panic caused Saul to disobey Samuel's specific instructions regarding the timing for battle. Instead of trusting and waiting on God's timing, Saul offered sacrifices to move the battle forward more quickly in direct violation of God's law that reserved this role for priests.

Samuel gave Saul the opportunity to confess and repent. Instead of humbling himself, Saul put forth excuse after excuse to justify his disobedience. This was only the beginning of Saul's problems, and God knew it. Saul's heart was far from God's. He repeatedly chose to do what was right in his eyes, rather than God's eyes. Samuel spoke hard words to Saul, *"You have done foolishly. You have not kept the command of the LORD your God, with which he commanded you"* (1 Samuel 13:13).

*04*     **Read 1 Samuel 13:13. What did Samuel say next?**

The word "foolish" here is not simply childlike foolishness. It means morally and spiritually lacking. So, though his act of disobedience may seem small, God saw into Saul's heart. Saul was a man who sought after Israel's heart and to please God's people more than God. Here we again see misplaced longings. Saul longed for approval, power and authority and looked for it in the wrong places. He looked to man instead of God for each of these longings. And because of that, Saul lost everything, including his life.

*05*     **According to Samuel, what was God looking for in the next king? (1 Samuel 13:14)**

Though Saul would reign another 20 years, his kingdom would never be the same. Samuel assured him it was over and his kingdom would not continue. (1 Samuel 13:14)

But God! There is hope for God's people. God had not rejected Israel. He had not abandoned His people. He loved with an everlasting love. He would raise up another king. A better king. One with a heart like His. A heart that reflected His coming Kingdom and King, Jesus. Not a perfect heart. But a heart that sought to trust and obey God.

# David

## Samuel anointed David to replace Saul as king, which eventually led to the division of Israel.

*"So all the elders of Israel came to the king at Hebron, and King David made a covenant with them at Hebron before the LORD, and they anointed David king over Israel."*

### 2 SAMUEL 5:3

Today we meet the man after God's own heart, King David.

In 2 Samuel 5, David experienced the fulfillment of God's plan for him to take his rightful place as King of Israel.

Let's pause and reflect on what a momentous day this was. Fifteen years had passed since Samuel anointed David king. (1 Samuel 16:6-13) David spent many of those years running for his life from King Saul, probably wondering if he would ever serve as Israel's King.

After the tragic death of Saul and Jonathan, it was time for David to take his throne.

I noticed something rather remarkable about David that provides further evidence for why God chose David to be the people's next king. Rather than celebrate Saul's epic failures and his horrific death, David mourned. (2 Samuel 1:11-12) And, in that mourning, David composed a beautiful lament to honor both Saul and Jonathan, revealing his most tender, forgiving, beautiful heart.

Read David's lament in 2 Samuel 1:17-27.

*01*  What led David to respond this way to Saul's death? To focus on the good and to love rather than speak words of hatred and bitterness? What distinguished David's heart from Saul's? (1 Samuel 13:13-14)

*02* Read the following passages and share what it means to have a heart like God. Psalm 51 (written by David after Nathan confronted him about his adultery with Bathsheba), Psalm 34:1-3 (written by David), 2 Samuel 21:1, 2 Kings 23:23-25, 2 Chronicles 16:9, John 14:15 and Acts 13:22.

*03* What instruction did God give to Samuel as he chose the king to follow Saul? (1 Samuel 16:7)

Initially, David only ruled over part of Israel, the house of Judah, because the commander of Saul's army made Saul's son, Ish-bosheth, king over Israel. His reign lasted seven years. Over those years, David grew stronger as Saul's son grew weaker and weaker.

In time, and after much strife and battle, the tribes of Israel turned to David and agreed he should be king. At that time, all 12 tribes were united again, as they were under Saul. Samuel tells us David was 30 years old when he took the throne.

*04* Who else was 30 years old when He began His ministry? Read Luke 3:23.

05 | Read 1 Chronicles 12:23-39 to get a wonderful picture of this monumental day in Israel's history. Does this remind you of another coronation day and great feast that is yet to come? (Isaiah 25:6-9)

One of my favorite parts of David's story is how this young shepherd boy, overlooked and rejected by so many, was chosen and appointed by God to be the earthly king who would lead His people.

Rejection is hard, but it doesn't have to destroy us. When we place our longings and desires fully in God's hands, rejection is actually a gift. God uses it to shape us into the women and men He created us to be. David's journey from shepherd boy to reigning king provides powerful truths and promises we can cling to today and every day.

King David reminds us that God alone provides the security we so desperately long for. He offers it to those who seek refuge in Him:

> For who is God, but the LORD?
> And who is a rock, except our God?
> This God is my strong refuge and
> has made my way blameless. He made
> my feet like the feet of a deer and
> set me secure on the heights.
>
> 2 SAMUEL 22:32-34

# This journey through Joshua, Judges and 1 and 2 Samuel, though hard to read at times, should bring us great encouragement about the character of our God.

Through these stories, we experience God's unconditional love, unending patience and abiding faithfulness to watch over and protect His people. Yes, He exacted punishment and issued consequences. But, in the end, God brought His people into their promised inheritance, into a place of safety, security and rest, and gave them a good king to lead them.

God will do the very same for us today because our God is the same yesterday, today and forever. He is still loving, patient, faithful and trustworthy. But, we make the journey so much easier when we walk closely with Jesus, aligning our hearts, our longings and our dreams with His. When we walk in the fullness of His love, mercy and grace.

Take a few minutes to sit with the truths and promises shared below. Let them soak into your heart and mind. Remember they are from the heart of the God who created you, formed and shaped you, and has your name engraved on the palm of His hand.

*God is faithful.*

*God is Sovereign.*

*Nothing can thwart His plans.*

*His plans are always good, even when you cannot see it.*

*God will never leave you or turn His back on you.*

Are you walking in a valley or wandering in the wilderness, wondering what God is doing or if He even hears or sees you? Join me in declaring those truths and promises over your circumstances today.

# God, thank You that You are sovereign

over the circumstances I am walking through. Thank You for David's story that shows me nothing can ever thwart Your plans. You are a faithful God. Your plans are always good, even though I cannot always see it. I take comfort in knowing You will not leave me or forsake me. I find my security in You and You alone because You are trustworthy. I commit in this moment to trust You and love You with my whole heart. I pray this in Jesus' name. Amen.

Samson delivered the Israelites from the Philistines.
JUDGES 13-15

The Lord provided Israel with judges to satisfy their longing for security from their enemies, but Israel did not listen to their judges.
JUDGES 2:18-19

The Israelites asked God for a king, which God said is a rejection of Him.

1 SAMUEL 8:7-18

David was anointed as king to replace Saul, which eventually led to the division of Israel.
2 SAMUEL 5:3

Boaz married Ruth and is a symbol of Christ, our kinsman redeemer.
RUTH

Gideon protected the Israelites from the kings of Midian.

JUDGES 6-8

God raised up Saul to be king, and he failed to seek God.
1 SAMUEL 9:16

David wrote many of the poems and songs we know as the Psalms.
(SEE ESPECIALLY PSALM 8, 19, 23, 51, 103 AND 139)

longing
for ——————————— *week four*
rescue

# One of the most stressful moments while driving may be when you hear the sirens of an ambulance or police car going off behind you.

As you pull over to the side of the road, you may have fleeting moments of wonder: Where are these first responders headed? What danger awaits them? Who is in need of help? We may offer prayers for those in need and hope what they are facing is not serious. We may wonder what the person in crisis may be feeling. The seconds may feel like hours while they wait in the pit of a crisis with a deep-down longing, hopeful that rescue is on its way.

While most of us are unsure of how to best help in traumatic emergencies, we're thankful for those trained to offer the exact help needed. First responders knowingly put themselves in harm's way because they are drawn to a greater need than that of protecting themselves. They are drawn to the reality that there is someone out there in desperate need of rescue. On some level, rescue is a feeling that may not be popular. If we say we need rescue, we're admitting that there is a crisis that we need rescue from. So, our acknowledgement of rescue is often nonexistent until we find ourselves in that pit. Then, it becomes an urgent ache that we hope will be resolved. God's people continually find themselves in need of rescue. Most often, because they put themselves in the pit of crisis trying to fulfill the deep-down soul desire that could only ever be truly satisfied by God.

This feeling of wanting to be rescued from our circumstances is a common human experience dating back to biblical times. In 1 Kings 17, the prophet Elijah faced persecution. He also suffered from a drought in the land brought on by the wickedness of King Ahab. Elijah's basic longing for food and physical protection was given to him by God who sent Elijah to the Wadi Cherith river so he could receive food from the ravens and drink from the river. A pattern we often find when it comes to God's rescue is that it often has a purpose other than what appears to be evident. God rescued Abraham so he could be an agent of rescue and a blessing to the nations. (Genesis 12:2) God rescued Elijah, so in turn Elijah could be an agent of God to show the foolishness of idolatry and the supremacy of God's divinity. (1 Kings 18) Throughout the books of 1 and 2 Kings and into the prophets ending with Malachi, we see that God intervenes on behalf of His people who often find themselves in the midst of crisis, longing for rescue. Yet, the kings and prophets all point to the final and full rescue that could only come in and through Jesus, the Son of God and rescuer and redeemer of mankind.

The images of crisis found in the Old Testament — from the oppression of Pharaoh, to the wilderness and the exile — are all shadows of the greatest evil: sin and its weapon, death. When we chase down every anxious feeling we have, its roots can be traced to our fear of the unknown, our fear of death or our fear of not being able to control other people and circumstances. God sent His son Jesus to enter humanity on a rescue mission. Christ on earth defeats the greater enemy — sin — on the cross, and in doing so, disarms the enemy's power, which is death, and reminds us God is ultimately in control. And when we trust Him, we have assurance beyond what we are facing. Christ's finished work on the cross is the answer to the soul ache for assurance, provision and the protection we all so desperately want.

We don't have to stand uncertain or anxious or fearful.

Our rescue is certain whether we experience it here on earth or not. Our eternal home is prepared and will make all that we temporarily face during our lifetime pale in comparison. That doesn't take away the pain of what we face now, but it sure does help us gain perspective that it won't always be this

way. The greatest hell a human can experience here on earth is not suffering. It's feeling like the suffering is pointless and will never get any better.[6] We don't ever have to fear that because our rescue from all that causes us to weep will end:

*"He will wipe away every tear from their eyes, and death shall be no more, neither shall there be mourning, nor crying, nor pain anymore, for the former things have passed away"* (Revelation 21:4).

What God the Father does for us in God the Son is a model for what you and I are called to do in the power of the Spirit of God who dwells within us. Just as Christ did, the rescuer must plunge into the human predicament in order to bring those in crisis to new life in Him. In the same way those first responders run toward the danger that awaits them because they are driven by a greater good, we must run toward those who are broken and battered, because we hold the good news of the gospel of a great God.

# North

NADAB    ELAH    OMRI    AHAZIAH

JEROBOAM I    BAASHA  ZIMRI    AHAB    JEHORAM

## Division of the Kingdom

DAVID   SOLOMON    930 B.C.

REHOBOAM   ASA    JEHORAM    ATHALIAH

ABIJAH   JEHOSHAPHAT  AHAZIAH   JOAS

# South

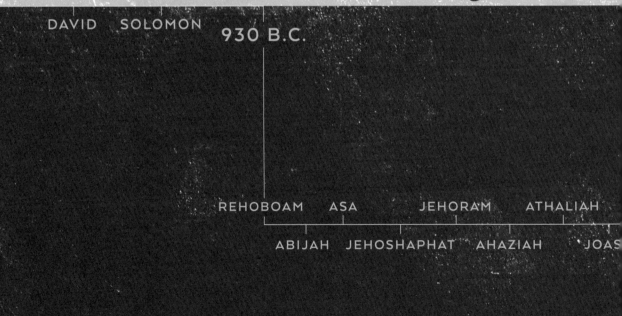

# Israel

JEHU    JEHOASH    ZECHARIAH    MENAHEM    PEKAH

JEHOAHAZ    JEROBOAM II    SHALLUM    PEKAHIAH    HOSHEA

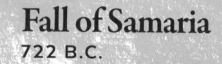

## Fall of Samaria
722 B.C.

## Fall of Jerusalem
586 B.C.

AMAZIAH    JOTHAM    HEZEKIAH    AMON    JEHOAHAZ    JEHOIACHIN

UZZIAH    AHAZ    MANASSEH    JOSIAH    JEHOIAKIM    ZEDEKIAH

# Judah

King Asa, in Judah,
renewed the covenant
with God's people.
2 CHRONICLES 14-16

During the corrupt reigns
of Ahab and Ahaziah in
Northern Israel, God
ministered through Elijah
and Elisha to lead the
charge for righteousness.

2 KINGS 2

David's son Solomon
was anointed king and
built the temple.
1 KINGS 1:39;1 KINGS 6

*Solomon wrote Ecclesiastes,
Song of Solomon and
many of the Proverbs.*

The prophet Hosea said that
God will call a people
*"Children of the living God"*
who were formerly called
*"Not My People."*
HOSEA 1-4

King Jehosaphat,
in Judah,
trusted God.
2 CHRONICLES 20

Israel was divided
between the
north and south.
1 KINGS 12:19

The prophet Amos condemned bribes and abuse of the poor.
AMOS 3-5

King Josiah, in Judah, renewed the covenant with God's people.
2 KINGS 23

# King Hezekiah, in Judah, trusted God.

## 2 CHRONICLES 29-32

The prophet Isaiah said there is a coming judgment for blind Israel and rescue through the Suffering Servant.
ISAIAH 1-2, 6, 53

The prophet Zephaniah said that the "Day of Lord" was near.
ZEPHANIAH 1

# The prophet Micah charged Judah to do justice and walk humbly.

## MICAH 1-2; 6:8

God had compassion on the Assyrians through the prophet Jonah.
JONAH

The prophet Jeremiah said Jerusalem would be destroyed because of Israel's disobedience.
JEREMIAH 1-5

Ezekiel saw visions of the presence of God leaving the temple as well as a future resurrection of God's people.
EZEKIEL 1-3, 18, 33

The prophet Joel warned people to turn from sin to God, and he foretold that one day, God's Spirit would be poured out on all people.
JOEL 2

The people of Israel mourned the fall of their holy city, Jerusalem.
LAMENTATIONS

Habakkuk predicted that Babylon would judge Judah but that the righteous would live by faith.
SEE ACTS 2;
HABAKKUK 1-2

Nahum taught the people to trust God and to believe Him, especially in times of great trouble or despair.
NAHUM 1

The cities of both Samaria in the North and Jerusalem in the South fell, and the people of Israel were exiled.
2 KINGS 17:6;
2 KINGS 25:1

**Haggai said** "Build God's house!"

Daniel had visions of the future, including end times and the resurrection of the dead.
DANIEL 10-12

An impatient Israel was told by God through Malachi to wait for a messenger, and 400 years of silence passed where no messenger of God spoke.
MALACHI 2:17-3:1

God demonstrated His sovereignty, providence and care, even for nations other than Israel.
ESTHER 7-8

God spoke through Obadiah about a day of judgment that is coming for all nations when they receive justice for all their deeds.
OBADIAH

Zechariah predicted the Christ riding on a donkey and that Jerusalem would be a blessing to *"All Nations."*
ZECHARIAH 9

Nehemiah, upbearer of Artaxerxes I, rebuilt the walls of Jerusalem.
NEHEMIAH 3-6

The temple was rebuilt but without its original grandeur.
EZRA 6:14

# God's People Move from a United Kingdom into a Divided Kingdom, to Exile and Captivity, to Reentry and Rebuilding

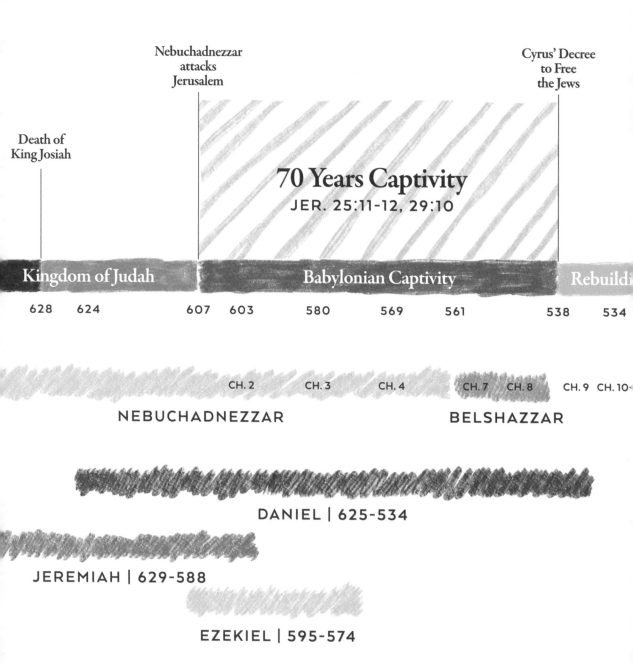

Nebuchadnezzar attacks Jerusalem

Cyrus' Decree to Free the Jews

Death of King Josiah

## 70 Years Captivity
### JER. 25:11-12, 29:10

Kingdom of Judah

Babylonian Captivity

Rebuildi

628    624                607    603        580        569        561            538        534

CH. 2        CH. 3        CH. 4        CH. 7    CH. 8        CH. 9    CH. 10

NEBUCHADNEZZAR                    BELSHAZZAR

DANIEL | 625-534

JEREMIAH | 629-588

EZEKIEL | 595-574

# Solomon

David's son Solomon was anointed king and built the temple.

---

*There Zadok the priest took the horn of oil from the tent and anointed Solomon.*
*Then they blew the trumpet, and all the people said, "Long live King Solomon!"*

1 KINGS 1:39

Though God called David a man after His own heart, (Samuel 13:14) some of David's sons did not live God-honoring lives. And sadly, none of his sons, not even Solomon who started off so well, followed God whole-heartedly.

David's son, Absolom, conspired and manipulated to overthrow his father — an extreme betrayal that led to Absalom's death. Yet, this could not have come as a surprise to David because Nathan prophesied this after David committed adultery with Bathsheba and ordered the murder of her husband, Uriah, to cover up his sin. (2 Samuel 12:11)

Near the end of David's days, he grew gravely ill. Another one of his sons, Adonijah, decided to take his father's throne without his father's knowledge or blessing. (1 Kings 1:5) Adonijah held his own coronation party and intentionally excluded all who opposed him. (1 Kings 1:5-10) The prophet, Nathan, informed King David of Adonijah's wrongful takeover and reminded him this was NOT God's plan. (1 Kings 1:27) King David made a sworn oath, reaffirming an earlier oath, that Solomon would be king. (1 Kings 1:30)

It's important to note that the idea of a co-regency — a king ruling alongside his son — was common during this time. David said Solomon would share his throne. (1 Kings 1:35) What Adonijah had done was not a co-regency but a mutiny, or betrayal.

*01* Read 1 Kings 1:5-27. **How would you describe Adonijah's attitude? Have you ever grown impatient with your circumstances or God's timing or just thought you knew better? Have you ever tried to force something that you didn't first bring to God in prayer? Describe how this played itself out in your life. In contrast, what are some ways we can seek the Lord with patience? (See Philippians 4:6)**

Doesn't this sound a bit familiar? Remember back in the garden? Adam and Eve, God's first children, also decided they knew better than their Father. God punished them for their disobedience by casting them out of the Garden. Since that time, God's people, including you and me, have been in need of **rescue.**

We see co-regency done well with Jesus. Jesus walked in perfect obedience with His Father's plan and now He currently shares the throne of heaven in complete harmony with His God and Father. (Revelation 5:13, Ephesians 1:3)

Nathan prophesied in 2 Samuel 7:12 that God would raise up offspring to succeed David and establish his kingdom. Solomon's inauguration was the first time Israel had ever received a king this way. The prophet Samuel anointed and appointed Saul and David as kings.

We cannot miss the significance of this moment ... God placing Solomon on the throne began the Davidic dynasty, the royal line that would eventually end in Jesus Christ, our rescuer.

David ordered Nathan to seat Solomon on King David's mule (1 Kings 1:33, 44) and escort him to his inauguration accompanied by trumpets, rejoicing and praises. (1 Kings 1:39)

If we look forward to John 12:12-19, we see a similar inauguration for another king. King Jesus. Jesus rode into the city of David on a donkey, accompanied by throngs of people singing, *"Hosanna! Blessed is he who comes in the name of the Lord! Blessed is the king of Israel!"* (John 12:13) The Jews and believers present would have known the history of God's people and would have recognized His parallels.

*02* | **How amazing is it the King of heaven would orchestrate history in such a way that we could recognize His Son when He walked the earth? How has this knowledge strengthened your faith in Christ? What feelings or emotions does this stir up in your heart?**

It's worth noting David's wisdom to include 1) Zadok, a priest, 2) Nathan, a prophet, and 3) Benaiah, the king's commander for the anointing of Solomon. It lent credibility to his kingship and validated Solomon's position as God's chosen king, not man's. This should cause us to stand in awe of God's love and power to write the story that ultimately brings humanity back to Eden. Solomon was not simply born to David; he was appointed and commissioned by God, and became a gift of grace to us all.

*03* | **Do you like being independent? I know I do. How might Solomon's commissioning lead you to rely on the people God has put in your life? What does it look like in your life to trust God and seek the counsel of godly people in the things you'd like to do?**

# Divided Kingdoms

Israel was divided between the North and South.

---

*"So Israel has been in rebellion against the house of David to this day."*

1 KINGS 12:19

Like us, Solomon was far from perfect. In fact, though we find Solomon's name in the lineage of Jesus, by his old age, Solomon defied God's rules and commands by marrying pagan women (women who did not worship the one true God) and following after their gods (violating God's very first commandment to have no other gods before Him). (1 Kings 11:1-2) I don't know about you, but this brings me great comfort that God would bless future generations through Solomon in spite of his sin.

| 01 | Consider times when you've disobeyed God. What consequences followed your disobedience? Has God used those consequences to rescue you? If so, how? What have you learned? |
|---|---|

In 1 Kings 11:12-13, the Lord clearly told Solomon that because of his sin, He would *"tear the kingdom away from"* Solomon except for one tribe (1 Kings 11:12). That is exactly what happened.

What happens next in Solomon's family can be quite confusing, so let's walk through it step by step. It's confusing because the two men who vie for kingship have very similar names: Jeroboam and Rehoboam. Rehoboam is Solomon's son ... his "real" son. Jeroboam was Solomon's chief servant and in charge of forced labor. So, remember "r" for "R"ehoboam, the "real" son. Got it? I promise it will help with the rest of the story.

Here is the account: A messenger of the Lord told Jeroboam he would receive 10 of the 12 tribes. (1 Kings 11:35-36) When Solomon heard this, he was angry and set out to kill Jeroboam, so Jeroboam fled to Egypt where he lived until Solomon died.

Upon Jeroboam's return, he went to Rehoboam (remember Solomon's "real" son and the rightful heir to the throne) and asked him to stop treating God's people so severely and instead treat them reasonably and compassionately. Jeroboam told Rehoboam if he would agree to this, he (Rehoboam) would have the people's loyalty. (1 Kings 12:4)

02 Consider how Jeroboam came and asked for peace despite previously being hunted like an animal. Have you sought reconciliation with your own enemies? Describe how this turned out.

Rehoboam sought counsel on how to respond to Jeroboam's request.

03 Read 1 Kings 12:6-11. From whom did Rehoboam seek advice, and what did they advise him to do? Whose advice did Rehoboam take?

04 Before we jump to what happens as a result of this division, who are some older men and women from whom you seek counsel? If you don't have any at this time, I encourage you to pray for God to bring a few into your life.

This battle between Rehoboam and Jeroboam forever changed Israel. Instead of one kingdom ruled by one king, it became two kingdoms. Rehoboam (grandson of David, son of Solomon, all three of whom were sons of Jesse from the tribe of Judah) ruled over the tribe of Judah, the southern kingdom. Jeroboam ruled over the remainder of the tribes in the north, known as the northern kingdom, also called Israel.

I hope you followed this complicated story. Please read 1 Kings 11 and 12 to get a better understanding of the story.

| 05 | **Have you ever done the good and right thing and suffered for it? If so, how did making that choice shape or impact your life? How did it affect your faith and trust in God?** |

What's hard about Scripture is we never know for certain what is happening in the hearts of the people in the stories. God relays the events as He wants us to know about them. We don't have commentary from God to accompany the Bible. But, we do know God's character. We know He is just. We know He is good. We know His purposes are good even if we can't "see" it or things don't work out in ways that seem "fair" to us. We have to trust God at His Word that He works all things together for good for those who love Him and are called according to His purpose. (Romans 8:28) There is always a bigger picture only God can see.

# Exile

The cities of both Samaria in the North and Jerusalem
in the South fell, and the people of Israel were exiled.

---

*"And in the ninth year of his reign, in the tenth month, on the tenth day of the month, Nebuchadnezzar king of Babylon came with all his army against Jerusalem and laid siege to it. And they built siegeworks all around it."*

2 KINGS 25:1

At this point in the story, we fast forward about 400 years — from the time Israel split around 930 B.C. to the time of the Babylonian exile. During this time, 19 kings ruled in the North and 19 kings in the South. At the end of nearly every king's reign, the author notes whether they were a good king or a bad king who did evil in the sight of the Lord. The northern kingdom produced no good kings. The southern kingdom had a few good kings like Asa and Josiah. But not a single Old Testament king would ever match the perfect righteousness and Kingship we see later in Jesus.

01 | Who are some heroes in your life? In what ways are these people like Jesus? In what way is Jesus even better?

The Assyrian empire defeated northern Israel. (2 Kings 17:6) This happened *"because the people of Israel had sinned against the LORD their God, who had brought them up out of the land of Egypt from under the hand of Pharaoh king of Egypt, and had feared other gods"* (2 Kings 17:7).

**02** By fearing and revering what was fake, the one true God gave them over to their fears to show them — and us — the folly in this. In what ways do you reserve your highest love and reverence for God alone?

About 100 years after the Assyrian captivity, the Babylonian empire stepped into the picture and conquered Assyria. They then marched into Jerusalem and burned it to the ground, destroying the temple, the royal palace and all the homes. They deported the Israelites, took some of the officials as prisoners, and executed others. They left the poorest of the poor to farm the land. They spared a mighty man named Daniel and deported him to Babylon to serve the king. You can read more about him in the biblical book bearing his name. They also deported a priest named Ezekiel who spoke for the Lord in Babylon.

We do find light in the midst of this dark time. Dark because the people had always had God with them. His presence literally lived among them in what was called "the Holy of Holies." First, in the tabernacle. Then, in the Temple. But, the Temple had been destroyed, and the people ripped from their homes and all that was familiar. Yet, God had not left them. He was still with them but not in a building. Now, God spoke to them through His called ones, through men like Daniel and Ezekiel. The news is even better for those of us who live after Jesus' birth. Eventually, God literally indwelled His people. His people, you and me, are now temples. His Spirit lives in us! (1 Corinthians 6:19)

**03** Have you ever felt like God was far away, like you can't feel, hear or see Him? How does what we've read today encourage you and help you find strength for today?

I'm so thankful we close our lesson today with one of God's "good" kings. His name is Josiah. He is the one who turned God's people back to the heart of God. Josiah found the Scriptures that had been hidden for generations of kings. He read it aloud from beginning to end in front of all God's people. He renewed the covenant God made with Abraham. He destroyed the altars to false gods. Most importantly, Josiah's sons, several generations later, led to Mary and Joseph and therefore Jesus, our Savior and *Rescuer*.

*04* | **Take some time to read 2 Chronicles 34:14-33. Share your observations on Josiah's reforms, as this is a very special part of the history of the kings.**

The history of the kings and the period of the exile reveal how faithful God is, even when we are not. God made a covenant with Abraham and kept His promises. It brings to mind 2 Timothy 2:13, *"if we are faithless, he remains faithful — for he cannot deny himself."*

*05* | **How does the faithfulness of God give you confidence to start your day? How does the fact that God is for you — your Rescuer, rooting for you — affect how you approach the circumstances of life?**

# Temple

The temple was rebuilt but without its original grandeur.

---

*"And the elders of the Jews built and prospered through the prophesying of Haggai the prophet and Zechariah the son of Iddo. They finished their building by decree of the God of Israel and by decree of Cyrus and Darius and Artaxerxes king of Persia."*

EZRA 6:14

The Israelite exiles felt lost and alone without the temple because they knew that as long as the temple was with them, God's presence was with them. But, in an instant, it was gone. Totally destroyed. But God. Knowing their hearts, God sent messengers to speak words of hope to sustain them.

*01* | **When you are discouraged, what encourages you?**

By this time, Persia had defeated Babylon and took over the entire region. But, a wonderful thing happened under this new regime: God gave the Israelites favor in the eyes of Babylon's leaders.

*"And the elders of the Jews built and prospered through the prophesying of Haggai the prophet and Zechariah the son of Iddo. They finished their building by decree of the God of Israel and by decree of Cyrus and Darius and Artaxerxes king of Persia"* (Ezra 6:14).

I always find it fascinating how consistently through history God used men in earthly governmental positions to accomplish His plans. One scholar, M. Breneman, addressed this by saying, "The most powerful word on earth at that time was the decree of a Persian king, but silently and mysteriously the king was being directed by an even more powerful divine word." [7]

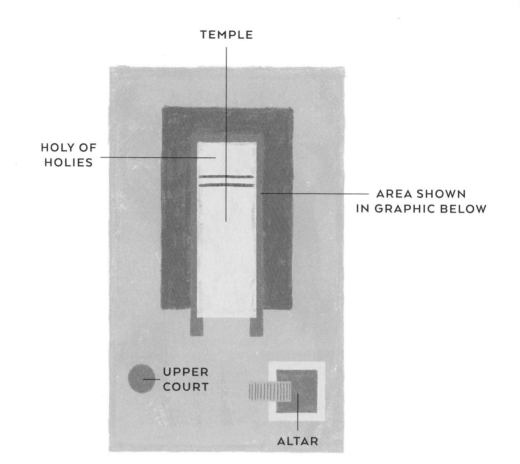

TEMPLE

HOLY OF
HOLIES

AREA SHOWN
IN GRAPHIC BELOW

UPPER
COURT

ALTAR

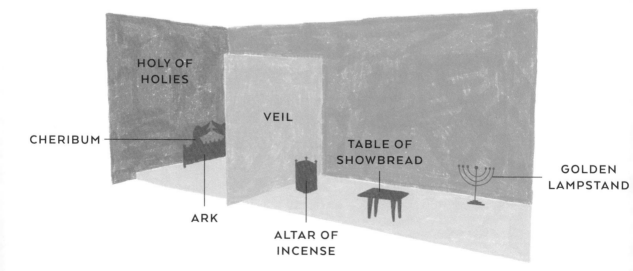

HOLY OF
HOLIES

VEIL

TABLE OF
SHOWBREAD

GOLDEN
LAMPSTAND

CHERIBUM

ARK

ALTAR OF
INCENSE

**02** What does this imply about how we should treat those who are in government and in authority over us?

The preaching and prophesying of Haggai and Zechariah, and the leadership and hard work of Zerubbable, Ezra and Nehemiah, led to the building of a magnificent new temple — a temple that survived in various forms, even through the Greek and Roman imperial takeovers.

What's so amazing is that hundreds of years before any of these events happened, Daniel dreamed about them. (Daniel 7) His dream centered around four beasts. The four beasts represented the four nations we just studied ... Babylon, Persia, Greece and Rome.

We've covered a lot of history in a short amount of time, and this truth seems clear: God used the visions, teachings and prophesying of Daniel, Ezekiel, Haggai and Zechariah to inspire and encourage the people to stand together and to work hard and persevere, even when hard times fell upon them and enemies surrounded them. God also used pagan kings to open doors and provide the means for the work to be done. And, best of all, God raised up three great leaders (Zerubbabel, Nehemiah and Ezra) who worked, served and led with a holy enthusiasm all Christians should share when they realize they are part of God's plan.

**03** How has the preaching of God's Word and/or the passion of those leading you affected your life? What are some of the ways you can see God's plan unfolding in your circumstances?

The second temple stood apart from the old one in one significant way. There is no evidence God's presence ever indwelled the second temple. Jesus' words in Revelation 21:22 reveal that there will be no temple in the new heaven and new earth because *"the Lord God Almighty and the Lamb"* are its temple. (see also Ezekiel 44:4, John 2:19) Yet, the very presence of the second temple encouraged God's people as they began their post-exile life together.

We are even more blessed than those who came before us. Instead of meeting God in a temple, His Holy Spirit now lives in those who call Jesus Lord and Savior. The Spirit of the Living God indwells every child of God! That is something to truly celebrate, my friend. We don't need anyone to open the door or give us access to God. Jesus did that when He gave His life for us. (1 Corinthians 3:16) We can meet with Him anytime, anywhere and any place. And, since Jesus is called the Word of God, (John 1:1) the first and best place to meet with Him each day is in the pages of Scripture, as we are doing throughout these 40 days.

*04* | **When, where and how do you meet with God?**

# Waiting

An impatient Israel was told by God through Malachi to wait for a messenger, and 400 years of "silence" passed, where no messenger of God spoke.

---

*"Behold, I send my messenger, and he will prepare the way before me. And the Lord whom you seek will suddenly come to his temple; and the messenger of the covenant in whom you delight, behold, he is coming, says the LORD of hosts."*

MALACHI 3:1

During the reign of Israel's kings, the glory of the Lord filled the temple. The people surely missed that.

*01* | Read 2 Chronicles 5:14 and describe what the glory of the Lord was like at that time.

This must have seemed confusing to God's people because Ezekiel's vision of the new temple reflected something so different. (Ezekiel 40-48) There are various thoughts on Ezekiel's temple that we don't have time to address here. Some say it was a literal temple that would be built on earth. Others say it was a figurative temple for one day in the future.

Ezekiel described a restored temple and the city of Jerusalem in a way that would have brought to mind the glory of Solomon's temple and one even greater. A time when God would again dwell with His people in perfect relationship. When and where, we simply do not know.

But what we do know is Jesus said one day He will raise up a new Temple. It would be His body, and it would be the place where the fullness of God is pleased to dwell. (Colossians 1:19)

I find great hope in both Ezekiel's words and Jesus' words. God did not, and has not, forsaken His people. He has restored our earthly relationship with Him in ways the Old Testament people could have never imagined. He will no longer just indwell a temple. He will indwell His people. Live in their very hearts. Make them become streams of living water! And, then one day, elevate them ... elevate us ... to a new glory and intimacy our minds cannot even conceive on this side of heaven.

*02*     **Read Malachi 2:17. What two things did the people do? Why did they do this?**

God gave the people one last prophet. And, after that prophet, God did not speak to His people for 400 years. Through Malachi, God told the Israelites again, as He did through Isaiah, to watch for a messenger in the wilderness. *"A voice cries: 'In the wilderness prepare the way of the LORD; make straight in the desert a highway for our God'"* (Isaiah 40:3).

In that time, it was not uncommon for messengers to prepare the way. Kings would send messengers ahead of them to remove any obstacles in the road to prepare for their coming.

Jesus and the gospel writers identified John the Baptiser as the messenger about whom Malachi spoke. (Matthew 3:3;11:7-10; Mark 1:3; Luke 3:4; John 1:23)

About 400 years passed between Malachi's prophecy and the births of John and Jesus. In fact, Jesus literally entered the temple as Malachi said He would in Malachi 3:1. ( Luke 2:21-40)

*03*     **Four hundred years is a long time to wait. However, what are some good things for which you have waited and received, or still wait? How do you stay patient in the waiting?**

There will be times that our ever-present God will seem far away, even hidden. But, He is still near even when we cannot feel His presence. Sometimes He remains silent because we are walking outside His will, walking in disobedience to something He's asked or expected of us. It can serve as a warning to us. To stop and listen. To spend intentional quiet time with Him so we can hear His voice or sense His leading or receive His redirection.

Remember Moses' words to God, "... If your presence will not go with me, do not bring us up from here" (Exodus 33:15). Moses wanted God's blessing and power to be with them because he knew he would otherwise fail. We too need to invite God into our lives, our plans and our prayers.

We've also talked about another way God is with us: through His presence living in us. Before Jesus' death and resurrection, the Holy Spirit rarely indwelled God's people. God sent His Spirit to empower those whom He called to particular tasks, like certain kings, judges and prophets. God also sent His presence to go before and behind His people as He led them in the wilderness and in battle. But, it was not until the New Testament, until the book of Acts, that God poured out His Spirit to live within His people.

I hope you know this by the end of this week's lessons: If you've placed your trust in Jesus, God lives in you. (1 Corinthians 3:16) Jesus said He would never leave us, (Hebrews 13:5) but that He would always be with us. (Matthew 28:20) He has never left you, and He will always be with you. Even now, in this very moment, HE IS WITH YOU!

*04* | **Do you believe the last four words you read? If you do, what impact does knowing this truth have on your life? If you don't believe those last words, or you aren't sure, ask God to show you. Invite Him to show you in very personal and specific ways that He is with you ... through prayer, through His Word, through worship. He will be faithful, my friend. He must be. It is who He is. He is a faithful God.**

# From the time of the kings, to the exile and destruction of Jerusalem, to the rebuilding of the new temple, mankind has longed for rescue.

When left to ourselves, we look for rescue through tangible things — people, institutions, things we can see and feel. Many are good gifts and provision from God. But, only God can rescue us from the mess we've made on earth. Thankfully, God's story, His Word, speaks wisdom and truth into this mess. Romans 15:4 says, *"For whatever was written in former days was written for our instruction, that through endurance and through the encouragement of the Scriptures we might have hope."* God's Word gives and brings true hope when it may feel that there is none.

God went before His people in a pillar of cloud by day and a pillar of fire by night. (Exodus 13:22) God remained with His people in the Holy of Holies in the temple. (1 Samuel 4:4) Both visual evidence of God. God was "with" them. Yet, I am reminded of Jesus' words in John 20:29, *"Have you believed because you have seen me? Blessed are those who have not seen and yet have believed."* There is more to God than we will ever be able to see with our eyes.

It's always been God's intention to *"dwell with man on the earth"* (2 Chronicles 6:18). He walked with us in the Garden of Eden and intends to walk with us again when He returns. But when we see God in heaven, however grand His glory will be on that day, the face we look at will be none other than the face of Jesus. *"He is the image of the invisible God, the firstborn of all creation. For by him all things were created, in heaven and on earth, visible and invisible, whether thrones or dominions or rulers or authorities—all things were created through him and for him. And he is before all things, and in him all things hold together"* (Colossians 1:15-17).

# Heavenly Father, thank You

for holding up a mirror to our own hearts as we read about Your people in the past. We long to see You and be with You in greater ways. We often long for rescue, perhaps by You, but adding whatever else it is we can see and hold on to. Help us to let go of hoping in anything else but You for life and godliness. In Jesus name, Amen.

# 400 years

of silence

# longing for

## for ——————— *week five*

## redemption

# When I was around nine years old, my mom took me to the toy store to go window shopping. *I hate window shopping!*

While we were out, I saw a Batman action figure that I really wanted, and I asked my mom if we could buy it. She said no, and I had a meltdown. But then, I did something I'm embarrassed to admit. When my mom wasn't looking, I put the toy in my pocket. In my mind, it was like the library, you know, I was "borrowing" the toy. But, we all know what I was really doing; I was stealing. It wasn't long before my mom found out what I did and boy, did I have a price to pay for my actions. Mom marched me back to the store, found the manager, made me apologize and hand over the Batman. I spent the next weekend "volunteering" at the store. My sin had a cost, and my mom made sure I paid it. What lesson did I learn? Every decision has a consequence. When I stuffed that figurine in my pocket, I had no idea the impact of my sin, not just on me but on those around me. We probably all have moments like that. And we also know, there is always a cost for sin and sometimes others have to pay the price for us.

Last week, we unpacked the longing for rescue and briefly covered the reality that one who rescues willingly places themselves at risk for the one who is rescued. A closely associated longing to rescue is redemption.

Rescue alone is incomplete when what remains is a divided and broken relationship. In that case, rescue requires redemption. True redemption comes at a price, and when that price is paid, redemption becomes a reality. It's important to remember, as my friend Lysa says, "While reconciliation may not always be possible with others, redemption with God is always possible." We've spent four weeks talking about what our longings are and how they drive us to act and think in certain ways, but this week, we make a shift as we consider what God longs for. As we've traced the story of God from Genesis, we know with assurance that God longs to be restored in right relationship with His people, (Matthew 23:37) and He actively works to achieve this. Throughout the Old Testament, the minor prophets anticipate a day when lasting redemption would be experienced by the people of God. The prophet Jeremiah uses words and phrases like, "the days are coming" or "in that day" or "at that time" with hopeful anticipation (Jeremiah 30:3, 8; 31:1). The prophet Zechariah sees redemption for the people of God in exile (Zechariah 10:8) and Isaiah promises that the people of God would be called "The Redeemed of the Lord" (Isaiah 62:12) because God would redeem the people from their sin. (Psalm 130:7-8)

Jesus made possible the redemption promised in the Old Testament and described in Psalm 130:7-8. As we enter the New Testament, the Gospels describe Jesus' death as a ransom for many. (Matthew 20:28; Mark 10:45) The English word "for" is the Greek word *"anti"* which can be translated "in place of" and speaks to the idea of substitution.

The ransom that was paid is an exchange that took place. The life of Christ for the life of humanity. C.S Lewis refers to this as "the great exchange," which required the shedding of Jesus' blood for the atonement of mankind. (Romans 3:24-25; Ephesians 1:7)

This exchange is a glorious reversal. Jesus' death not only frees humanity from the bondage of sin and death, it also redeems and restores our relationship with God. We are again sons and daughters of the King. (Galatians 4:6-7) That ache we feel in our hearts for redemption is an indication and reminder that we were never meant to live apart from God. The "good news" of the gospel is that Jesus opened the way for us to once again be in the presence of God. To be in relationship with Him. To live a redeemed life. One where we know we are fully loved, never again separated from our Creator.

# Here are both

Here are both of the genealogies of Jesus given to us by Matthew and Luke, showing both Mary and Joseph's lineage. What is fascinating about Matthew's list is that he includes four women, all of whom were likely gentiles (non-Jews), and at least three of whom are known to have been involved in some kind of immorality. Instead of leaving them out, which would have been easier, by listing these women Matthew proudly shows that Jesus is both our God and Redeemer, full of grace and truth, who came to love and save sinners. Read Matthew 1:1-17 and fill the blanks showing how these women became the mothers of our King and Savior, Jesus Christ.

GOD
ADAM
SETH
ENOSH
CAINAN
MAHALALEL
JARED
ENOCH
METHUSELAH
LAMECH
NOAH
SHEM
ARPHAXAD
CAINAN
SHELAH
EBER
PELEG
REU
SERUG
NAHOR
TERAH
ABRAHAM
ISAAC
JACOB
JUDAH
PEREZ
HEZRON
RAM
AMMINADAB
NAHSHON
SALMON
BOAZ
OBED
JESSE
DAVID

14
generations
from
Abraham
to
David

Genealogy of Jesus — two parallel lines

Line via Solomon:

SOLOMON
REHOBOAM
ABIJAH
ASA
JEHOSHAPHAT
JORAM
UZZIAH
JOTHAM
AHAZ
HEZEKIAH
MANASSEH
AMON
JOSIAH
JECONIAH

SHEALTIEL
ZERUBBABEL
ABIUD
ELIAKIM
AZOR
ZADOK
ACHIM
ELIUD
ELEAZAR
MATTHAN
JACOB
JOSEPH
MARY

Line via Nathan:

NATHAN
MATTATHAH
MENAN
MELEA
ELIAKIM
JONAN
JONAN
JOSEPH
JUDAH
SIMEON
LEVI
MATTHAT
JORIM
ELIEZER
JOSE
ER
ELMODAM
COSAM
ADDI
MELCHI
NERI

SHEALTIEL
ZERUBBABEL
RHESA
JOANNAS
JUDAH
JOSEPH
SEMEI
MATTATHIAH
MAATH
NAGGAI
ESLI
NAHUM
AMOS
MATTATHIAH
JOSEPH
JANNA
MELCHI
LEVI
MATTHAT
HELI
JOSEPH

14 generations from David until captivity in Babylon

14 generations from captivity in Babylon until Christ

JESUS

The angels appeared
to the shepherds to
announce Jesus' birth.
LUKE 2:8-20

John's desert life
was recorded and
fulfilled a prophecy.
LUKE 3:1-20

Jesus and his family
fled to Egypt,
a fulfillment of
Jeremiah 31:15.
MATTHEW 2:13-18

John
and
Jesus'
birth
were
foretold.

LUKE 1:5-38

**Fulfilling our
longing for redemption,
Jesus, God the Son,
was born a man.**

MATTHEW 1:18-25;
LUKE 2:1-46

Jesus lived in Nazareth
and the favor of God
was upon Him.
LUKE 2:39-40

The Magi visited
the newborn
King of the Jews.
MATTHEW 2:1-12

**John baptized Jesus** *"to fulfill all righteousness."*

MARK 1:9-11;
MATTHEW 3;
LUKE 3

Jesus grew in wisdom and stature, and in favor with God and man.
LUKE 2:41-52

Jesus began gathering his first disciples.
JOHN 1:35-51

Jesus healed many people.
MARK 1:21-34

Jesus was tempted in the wilderness.
MATTHEW 4:1-11;
MARK 1:12-13;
LUKE 4:1-13

John denied being the Christ and told the world to behold the Lamb of God.
(Isaiah 40:3 fulfilled)
JOHN 1:19-34

Jesus turned water to wine in obedience to his mother as his first recorded miracle.
JOHN 2:1-11

Jesus healed the
centurion's servant
from afar, in response
to the centurion's faith.
LUKE 7:1-10

Jesus
called
12
of his
disciples
"apostles."

MARK 3:13-19

Jesus
calmed
the
storm.

MARK 4:35-41

Jesus cleansed
the temple
of corruption.
JOHN 2:13-22

Jesus revealed to
the woman at
the well that he
was the Christ,
and many believed
in Him that day.
JOHN 4:5-42

Jesus raised a
widow's son
to life.
LUKE 7:11-17

Jesus preached one of his
many sermons on the side
of a mountain that we
have come to know as the
"Sermon on the Mount."

MATTHEW 5-7; LUKE 6:20-49

Peter
confessed
that
Jesus
was the
Son of
God.

MATTHEW 16:13-20

Jesus was transfigured
and announced by the
Father to be His Son.
MARK 9:2-10;
LUKE 9:28-36;
MATTHEW 17:1-9

Jesus
raised
Lazarus
from
the
dead.

JOHN 11:1-44

Jesus foretold that He
would be rejected and killed,
and that He would rise
again on the third day.
MARK 8:31-7

Jesus fed 5,000 men,
and even more women
and children, by
miraculously multiplying
fish and bread.
JOHN 6:1-13

Large crowds followed
Jesus and He warned
them to count the cost.
Luke 14:25-35

# The Birth of Jesus

Fulfilling our longing for redemption, Jesus, God the Son, was born a man.

---

*"Now the birth of Jesus Christ took place in this way. When his mother Mary had been betrothed to Joseph, before they came together she was found to be with child from the Holy Spirit."*

MATTHEW 1:18

Our culture seems fascinated with discovering our ancestry — what country we're from and what our family's story is. In Jewish times, this was incredibly important as well because people gained certain rights and status based on the tribe into which they were born.

This is why Matthew opens his Gospel with a genealogy and the story of Jesus' birth. Matthew's entire message unfolds why Jesus is the one true King and Messiah. Matthew reminds us 16 times that Jesus came to fulfill the Old Testament prophecies. King David's bloodline brought us both Joseph and Mary. The prophecy from Isaiah 9:6-7 foretold the Messiah would come from the house of David.

*01* | Why do you think Matthew would choose to start with the genealogy of Jesus?

Matthew then told the story of Jesus' birth. It was time for the prophesied Son of God to make His grand entrance into this world. By the power of God, the Holy Spirit, the One who is fully God and fully man, confined Himself in the womb of a virgin named Mary. This amazing miracle fulfilled the prophecy in Isaiah 7:14.

| | |
|---|---|
| *02* | **Read Isaiah 7:14. Jesus' name is Immanuel which means "God with us." What does this mean for you that Jesus' name is Immanuel, God with *you*?** |

With the birth of Jesus, the Word became flesh and dwelt among us. (John 1:14) God's children needed redeeming. God, the Father, sent God the Son, Jesus, as the vessel for that redemption. Through that redemption, God provided a way for His children to fulfill the longings we've been exploring throughout these 40 days — both the longings they could identify and those they could not. For it was, as it still is, God's desire for His children to fulfill their longings in Jesus alone, not the things of this world.

# Baptism of Jesus

Jesus was baptized by John "to fulfill all righteousness."

*In those days Jesus came from Nazareth of Galilee and was baptized by John in the Jordan. And when he came up out of the water, immediately he saw the heavens being torn open and the Spirit descending on him like a dove. And a voice came from heaven, "You are my beloved Son; with you I am well pleased."*

MARK 1:9-11

## Prepare the way.

John the Baptist, Jesus' cousin, prepared the way for Jesus' arrival through baptism. (Isaiah 40:3) As believers, we continue to celebrate baptism as a sacred act to acknowledge our faith in Christ. Baptism is an outward, visible sign of the inward workings that the Holy Spirit of God is doing within us.

*01* | **Jesus *allowed* John to baptize Him. Why did Jesus choose to be baptized?**

By submitting to baptism, Jesus connected with mankind and demonstrated our need to both bury and be cleansed from our sins.

Matthew writes that as John baptized Jesus, the heavens opened and the Spirit of God descended like a dove and rested upon Jesus. (Matthew 3:16) Let's pause and take in the significance of this moment. It's one of the few times we explicitly witness the Trinity working together in Scripture. God the Father spoke, God the Son was baptized, and God the Holy Spirit descended.

God spoke these powerful words, "This is my beloved Son" (Matthew 3:17). These carefully chosen words ensured that all who witnessed the baptism knew Jesus was not a common man.

*02*  God again identifies Jesus as His beloved Son. What is the name of that event? (See Matthew 17)

Scripture speaks of another significant baptism in Acts 8. Let's travel there.

Early in Acts (this was after Jesus' death and resurrection), the 12 apostles chose a man named Philip to be one of seven men to carry out practical and administrative duties for the church. Philip left Jerusalem and traveled to Samaria, an area avoided by most Jews. While evangelizing there, the angel of the Lord came to Philip and told him to travel south on a particular road. Philip obeyed and, along the way, found an Ethiopian Eunuch sitting in his chariot on the side of the road. He was reading from the book of Isaiah, seeking to understand its meaning. Philip joined him, opened the Scriptures for him and shared the good news about Jesus. (Acts 8:35) At one point, they came across a body of water and the Ethiopian asked what prevented him from being baptized. Philip took him down to the water and baptized him. As they came out of the water, the Spirit carried Philip away, and the Ethiopian man went away rejoicing! God had revealed Truth to him and welcomed him into the family of God. Hallelujah! What a beautiful picture.

Let's return to Jesus' baptism. You'll notice an unusual thing happened. After this heavenly ordained moment, instead of celebrating and rejoicing, God the Spirit sent God the Son into isolation ... into the wilderness.

*03*  Why do you think God timed Jesus' baptism just before going into the wilderness?

# Temptation of Jesus

Jesus was tempted in the wilderness.

---

*"And Jesus, full of the Holy Spirit, returned from the Jordan and was led by the Spirit in the wilderness for forty days, being tempted by the devil. And he ate nothing during those days."*

LUKE 4:1-2

Remember the question we ended with yesterday? Why did God time Jesus' baptism just before He sent Him into the wilderness? Because God knew what lay ahead for Jesus. Read the words that open Luke 4, Jesus was *"full of the Holy Spirit;"* (Luke 4:1). Jesus' baptism equipped, filled, armed and readied Him for the 40 days of tempting he was about to encounter.

As a point of interest, you might notice the number 40 mentioned here. This number holds significance throughout Scripture.

*01* | **Where else do we find the number 40? Read Genesis 7:12 (Noah and the ark). Read Numbers 32:13 (the Israelites in the wilderness). Read Acts 1:3 (Jesus' appearance after His resurrection).**

Jesus fasted during those 40 days. Because Jesus set the example of fasting, let's take a moment to learn about it. Biblical fasting required abstaining from food, and sometimes water. The purpose of fasting is to abstain from physical food and instead focus on filling ourselves with spiritual food. How do we "fill" ourselves? Spending time with Jesus, the One who is the Bread of Life and Living Water. What does this look like? Reading our Bibles, praying and worshiping God through song, to name a few.

It's clear from reading Jesus' words back to Satan that Jesus had His Father's words hidden in His heart. Jesus combated each temptation with Scripture and used it as a weapon against Satan. Jesus didn't engage in discussion with Satan. He simply spoke forth God's Word.

**02** Let's go to Ephesians 6 to learn more about this weapon. Specifically read verses 10-18. Looking at 6:17, what does Paul call the Word of God? List out the other pieces of armor below.

Let's pause for a moment and set forth one very significant truth. While the enemy is a deceiver, manipulator, thief and accuser, he is not supreme. He is no match for God. God is the Creator; Satan is the created one. No created being is ever greater than its Creator. Jesus knew this and confidently declared the Word to keep the enemy in his rightful place.

**03** Just as Jesus was filled with the Holy Spirit, (Luke 4:1) so are we. (John 14:16; Ephesians 1:13) How will these truths, and this event, impact you the next time you suspect Satan is attempting to deceive and manipulate you?

**04** Where else do we see the enemy twist the words of God? Read Genesis 3.

While Satan's wilderness temptations were specific to Jesus, the longings behind those temptations apply to us as well.

The Devil used the same tactics against the second Adam (Jesus) that he used against Adam and Eve in the garden of Eden.

Satan presented stones to Jesus to turn into bread, appealing to physical satisfaction (the lust of the flesh). In our lives, this may sound like: *God is not going to provide what I need so I need to take this situation into my own hands and maintain control.*

Satan took Jesus to the top of the temple, to **see** all the kingdoms, appealing to the desire to gain power (the lust of the eyes). We might say it this way: *I'm not satisfied with what I have and God won't give me what I desire, so I'll take it myself.*

Satan tempted Jesus to call on the angels to save Him, appealing to pride and the desire to appear important (the pride of life). He was, afterall, the Son of God. Pride says: *God is not giving me what I deserve, so I'll grasp it for myself.*

# Our Longings Haven't Changed

| Scripture | Who is tempted | Physical/ Satisfaction | Mental / Possessions | Emotional / Significance |
|---|---|---|---|---|
| Genesis 3:6 | Eve | "So when the woman saw that the tree was good for **food**..." | "...and that it was a delight to the **eyes**..." | "...and that the tree was to be desired to make one **wise**..." |
| Luke 4:3-10 | Jesus | "...command this stone to become **bread**..." | "...the devil took him up and **showed** him all the kingdoms of the world..." | "...He will command his angels **concerning you,** to guard you..." |
| 1 John 2:16 | Everyone | "For all that is in the world— the desires of the **flesh**..." | "...and the desires of the **eyes**..." | "...and **pride of life**—is not from the Father but is from the world." |

Jesus' response to Satan's temptations gives us tools to fight with today when feelings of fear, isolation and rejection overwhelm us. We do not fight alone, but with the power of the Holy Spirit and the Word of God, knowing Jesus went before us all in this fight.

*05* | Do you have certain scriptures you say aloud or go to in times of trouble? If so, list one or two here. If not, consider reading and copying one of these: Romans 8:35-39; 1 John 4:4; Isaiah 54:17.

# Sermon on the Mount

Jesus preached one of His many sermons on the side of a mountain
that we have come to know as the "Sermon on the Mount."

*"And when Jesus finished these sayings, the crowds were astonished at his teaching,
for he was teaching them as one who had authority, and not as their scribes."*

MATTHEW 7:28-29

Think of a time you witnessed a new president or political figure take office. Many people watch inaugural addresses, eager to hear the new leader's vision for the future and the heart behind why he or she has chosen the high calling of leadership.

In Matthew 5, instead of a political leader, we find Jesus declaring His vision and purpose for His people. Instead of news anchors standing ready to narrate with cameras pointed at Jesus, we find His core disciples close by, and crowds gathering around to listen.

Theologian David Guzik compares the words Jesus spoke that day in His Sermon on the Mount to the United States' Declaration of Independence. Just as Thomas Jefferson and the founding fathers declared the purpose of the forming government and the rights secured through it for the new nation, Jesus spoke His words to usher in His new Kingdom and declared what

it would look like to live as His follower and serve as a member of God's Kingdom. He aimed to show how worshiping Him as the King of kings and Lord of lords translated into new ways of believing, thinking and acting.

Matthew opens Chapter 5 by telling us, *"And [Jesus] opened his mouth and taught them"* (Matthew 5:2). Jesus first taught the Beatitudes found in Matthew 5:1-11. Beatitudes means a condition or state of blessedness. One scholar said it can also be understood as giving a believer "be-attitudes."[ [8] These are attitudes he or she should be ... or have. I love that! They are spiritual attributes Jesus values in our character. None of them come naturally. We can only live them through the power of Jesus alive in us through His Holy Spirit. When we walk in these attributes, God promises abundant spiritual blessings.

*01* | Take some time to read the Beatitudes in Matthew 5:1-11. Remember, the Beatitudes are the attitudes we should "be." Which attitude do you feel needs improvement in your own life and what steps will you take to implement the attitude you just identified?

In Matthew 5:13-16, Jesus declared who we are ... *"salt of the earth"* and *"light of the world."*

02 | **What does it mean to you personally to be a light to the world? Have you had a time in the past where you've been someone's light? How did God use this in your life and theirs?**

Take a moment and pray for an opportunity to be a light to someone today! To bring hope into their despair. Laughter into their sadness. Full into their empty. Kindness into their grumpiness (I know this is hard). May God bless and reward you in tangible ways as you seek to live according to His Kingdom purposes today!

This next passage sets forth Jesus' authority: *"Do not think I have come to abolish the Law or the Prophets; I have not come to abolish them but to fulfill them"* (Matthew 5:17). When Jesus set forth these radical changes, He spoke with authority as the Son of God, the Son in whom God said He was well pleased. His words commanded more attention because of *who* He was.

03 | **Read Luke 24:44-45 and Romans 8:3-4; 10:4. According to these passages, how do the law and prophets relate to Jesus?**

Throughout the rest of the teaching on the Sermon on the Mount, Jesus contrasted the characteristics of a true believer with the hypocrisy of the religious people, especially the Jews and the Pharisees, who lived and breathed law and works and judged everyone by their standards. Jesus' purpose and passion was to move people from law and works to love and grace that produce righteous works — to lead His people from self-centeredness to other-centeredness. He knew the depths of our depravity because He was one of us, yet was still perfect in humanity and divinity. He knew how our flesh would long for the attention, approval and admiration of others. But Jesus also knew that praise and admiration would ring empty every time and never fulfill our deepest needs and longings. Those will only ever be satisfied in giving all of ourselves to Jesus!

# The Transfiguration

Jesus was transfigured and announced by the Father to be His Son.

---

*"And after six days Jesus took with him Peter and James and John,*
*and led them up a high mountain by themselves. And he was transfigured before them."*

MARK 9:2

About a week after Jesus predicted his death, He invited three of his disciples to witness a spectacular miracle called the transfiguration. "Transfigure" is a word translated from the Greek *metamorphoō* meaning to transform. Jesus led the three up a high mountain, isolated from everyone else, and was transfigured before their eyes. Matthew tells us, *"[Jesus'] face shone like the sun, and his clothes became white as light"* (Matthew 17:2). Those disciples beheld God's glory! Can you imagine? Remember, Jesus is fully God and fully human. At this moment in time, God let His glory shine forth like the radiant sun through Jesus.

To be honest, Matthew 17 intimidates me. I think I would have done exactly what Peter, James and John did. Scripture tells us they fell on their faces and were terrified. (Matthew 17:6)

And, if that wasn't stunning enough, appearing with Jesus were Moses and Elijah. They were hanging out, having a conversation just steps away from Peter, James and John. Imagine what that must have been like. This was a powerful, pivotal moment in Scripture where we witness Jesus reveal the fullness of His divinity to the disciples. Not only is He transfigured before their eyes, but Moses and Elijah appear!

Moses had lived some 1,400 years before and Elijah 900 years, yet there they were talking with Jesus in resurrected, glorified bodies. I especially love that Moses was there. Remember when we saw him last? It was on top of Mount Nebo. God told him he would not enter into the Promised Land. It broke our hearts.

Read Deuteronomy 34:1-5 to refresh your memory.

Moses, the giver of the law, does plant his feet in the Promised Land. Though God did not allow Moses to walk into Canaan, He does fulfill his destiny. God's promise does come true. But, it's in an exceedingly greater way than Moses could have ever imagined. Jesus himself brings Moses in.

Elijah is there too. Remember Elijah, the prophet of God?

Read 2 Kings 2:1-11 to refresh your memory about Elijah.

01 | Having read the Deuteronomy and 2 Kings passages, what is the significance of Moses and Elijah appearing?

Moses, the one who faithfully led the Israelites out of Egypt, represented the law while Elijah, called up to heaven without death, represented the prophets. The sum total of Old Testament revelation stood before the three disciples. The two who best represented the law and the prophets that Jesus repeatedly claimed He fulfilled. The presence of these two glorified people validated what Jesus was teaching.

Again, another miracle happens, one that takes us back to Jesus' baptism.

02 | Read Matthew 17:4-8 and Matthew 3:16-17. What enveloped them? Who spoke and what did He say about Jesus?

03 | **Who was left standing by the end of Matthew 17:8?**

Oh, friend, Jesus' disciples didn't fall to the ground, even after all those miraculous events they witnessed, until they heard the voice of God speaking. Only then did they fall facedown to the ground. God wanted to ensure that they knew to the depths of their soul that Jesus was the Messiah. He was who He said He was.

Why was Jesus the only one left? Because He was enough. Moses (the law) and Elijah (the prophets) have passed. Only Jesus remained!

Jesus had just predicted His death. When Jesus spoke those words in Matthew 16, Peter said, *"Never, Lord! This shall never happen to you!"* (Matthew 16:22) God used this mountaintop experience to prepare them for that day. For the crucifixion. When it would feel like their world was falling apart and all hope was lost, they could remember this moment. The hope of Jesus as the Living God. The true Messiah. The hope of the resurrection of the dead, as evidenced by Moses and Elijah.

And, here is an amazing truth for us: One day, after our death, we too will be resurrected. We too will hang out with Jesus. We'll talk with Jesus. We'll see Him not just as a man we read about in the Bible, but we'll see Him transfigured in glorious power in dazzling white. I cannot wait for that day!

# This week, the King of kings made His grand entrance.

Through the birth of Jesus and the beginning of His ministry, the Redeemer of the world came to permeate the places in our hearts where our hurts, desires and needs reside. Since we entered into this world, we innately have a longing within us. A desire and need to be seen, validated and praised. Because of Jesus, we don't have to strive to fill that need with praise from man and/or earthly possessions. Jesus is our daily bread. He is the light of the world. His is the only One worthy to receive praise. He lived a life we could not live. He redeemed what was lost and broken.

The crowds began to follow Jesus in the Gospels, and today we have the same opportunity to follow Him. Because as we learned this week:

*The poor in spirit receive the kingdom of heaven.*
*Those who mourn shall be comforted.*
*The meek will inherit the earth.*
*Those who hunger and thirst for righteousness will be satisfied.*
*Those who are merciful will receive mercy.*
*Those who are pure in heart shall see God.*
*Peacemakers will be called sons of God.*

Friend, we can rejoice and be glad to know any hurt or persecution we feel today was felt by the generations who came before us. Revelation 21:4 tells us, *"He will wipe away every tear from their eyes, and death shall be no more, neither shall there be mourning, nor crying, nor pain anymore, for the former things have passed away."* Glory be to God!

*Today, I encourage you to find a quiet place and pray the Lord's Prayer from Matthew 6. As you begin, notice the words Jesus speaks before He gives the actual prayer.*

# But when you pray, go into your room and shut the door

*and pray to your Father who is in secret. And your Father who sees in secret will reward you ... for your Father knows what you need before you ask him. Pray then like this:*

*"Our Father in heaven, hallowed be your name. Your kingdom come, your will be done, on earth as it is in heaven. Give us this day our daily bread, and forgive us our debts, as we also have forgiven our debtors. And lead us not into temptation, but deliver us from evil.*

*For if you forgive others their trespasses, your heavenly Father will also forgive you, but if you do not forgive others their trespasses, neither will your Father forgive your trespasses"* (Matthew 6:6-15). Amen.

# longing for fulfillment

*week six*

# Promises are tricky — especially because we make promises with every intention to follow through and fulfill them.

My kids are the promise police. They have a very special gift to recall every promise I've ever made them and then call me out on any promise that I don't follow through on — especially when it comes to dessert. One morning, I promised the kids Oreos for dessert that evening. After dinner, I realized we had no Oreos in the house. Not even Oreo crumbs. I knew I would have a revolt on my hands that would begin with my kids reminding me, "But dad, you promised!" Why were my kids so devastated by the loss of the Oreos? It's because my promise to my children comes with authority, trust, expectation and vulnerability. My kids see me as Dad, and that name, that role, carries with it a special authority that provides security. That security establishes trust. The promise also sets an expectation for what is anticipated. They trust my promise will be fulfilled, and that trust leaves my kids in a vulnerable position: They are longing and waiting for a promise to be fulfilled based on trust and assurance. Just like my kids, we often find ourselves in a similar position where we have received a promise yet live in the *not yet* of its fulfillment.

As we enter Week 6 of our study, we've come across many of God the Father's promises to His children.

1. **God promised to restore and redeem humanity after the Fall. (Genesis 3:15)**

2. **God promised to bless Abraham, make him into a great nation and bless the nations through him. (Genesis 12:2; 15:5-6; 17:4-6)**

3. **God promised to provide His children land and an inheritance. (Exodus 3:17)**

4. **God promised rescue, redemption and restoration to the Israelites yet in exile. (Jeremiah 30:3, 8; 31:1; Zechariah 10:8; Isaiah 62:12)**

After so much waiting and living in the silence of unfulfilled promises, fulfillment came; His name, Jesus. One of the most important things we learn about God and His ways is that God is so much higher and bigger than us, and His ways are not our ways. God chose to bring fulfilment in the most unexpected, yet glorious way. There was never a plan B, only a plan A, and every second from the fall of mankind was leading up to the arrival of God the Son. However, God is not motivated by what we think is best, but what He knows is best. The Israelites expected a conquering king who would rescue them from the hands of their Roman enemies. They received the Suffering Servant and Prince of Peace who rode into Jerusalem on a donkey, which itself is a symbol of peace. (Matthew 21:1-11; Mark 11:1-11; Luke 19:28-44; John 12:12-19) Jesus would in fact conquer, but He would conquer sin and death, the greater enemy of humanity, and disarm the evil powers.

The people longed for the fulfillment of the promise made to their forefather Abraham. In Acts 2, God gives the Spirit of God to indwell all people that submit and place their faith, hope and trust in Jesus. The disunity of Babel in Genesis 11 is reversed in Acts 2. At Babel, (Genesis 11:1-9) humanity was first genuinely divided. The expression of the division was through different languages which we see as God's judgment for the wickedness of man. However, what took place at Pentecost (Acts 2) is an indication that the disunity of people has been divinely reversed by the power of the Spirit. The Spirit gives a common understanding of languages despite the differences that may exist. [9] Finally, the multi-ethnic family promised to Abraham comes into fulfillment. In each of these instances, we see the beauty and goodness of God who is faithful to His promises because He is our good Father, worthy of our trust and vulnerability. He is faithful even when we are faithless. (2 Timothy 2:13)

## Jesus rode into Jerusalem on a donkey as a king in what is known as The Triumphal Entry.

JOHN 12:12-19;
MATTHEW 21:1-11;
MARK 11:1-11;
LUKE 19:28-44

Jesus publicly denounced the teachers of the Jewish law.
MATTHEW 23;
LUKE 11:37-54

## Jesus predicted His crucifixion, the harshest of punishments.

MATTHEW 26:1-5

## Jesus made a fig tree wither and cleansed the temple again.

MATTHEW 21:12-22;
MARK 11:12-26

Jesus predicted the fall of Jerusalem and His second coming.
MATTHEW 24-25;
MARK 13;
LUKE 21:5-36

Judas was upset with Jesus for allowing Mary to "waste" ointment on Himself.
JOHN 12:1-8

Jesus established the
sacrament of communion.
MATTHEW 26:26-29;
1 CORINTHIANS 11:23-26

Jesus was examined by
Caiaphas the High Priest.
JOHN 18:12-14; 19-23

Jesus
washed
*all* of his
disciples'
feet,
even
Judas.

JOHN 13:1-21

## Jesus ate His last supper and was betrayed by Judas.

JOHN 13;
MATTHEW 26;
MARK 14;
LUKE 22

Jesus prayed for escape,
and the will of God,
and was arrested in the
Garden of Gethsemane.
MARK 14:26; 32–46

## Jesus was tried by the Sanhedrin.

MATTHEW 26:57

Peter denied knowing
his Lord three times
as Jesus said he would.
MARK 14:54; 66-72

Jesus went before
Pilate again, who
finally ordered Jesus
to be killed out of
fear of an uprising.
MATTHEW 27:15-26

Jesus went before
Pontius Pilate and
was found not guilty.
JOHN 18:28-38

Judas
took his
own life.

MATTHEW 27:3-10

Jesus
was
crucified
on the
cross.

LUKE 23:32-46;
MATTHEW 27;
MARK 15;
JOHN 19

Jesus went before
Herod Antipas and
was found not guilty.
LUKE 23:6-12

Jesus was buried
in the tomb of
Joseph of Aramithea
after being speared
through His side.
MATTHEW 27:57-60;
JOHN 19:31-42

A group
of women
reported the
empty tomb
but were
not believed.
LUKE 24:1-12

Three hours of
darkness and
other strange
things occurred.
MATTHEW 27:45-56;
MARK 15:33-41;
LUKE 23:44-49

There
was a
great
earthquake.
MATTHEW 28:1-4

Jesus appeared
to more than
500 people.
1 CORINTHIANS 15:6

Jesus
walked
and
ate
with
His
disciples.
LUKE 24:15; 41-43

The Holy Spirit came,
as promised, to dwell
inside all believers
in Christ.
ACTS 1:8; 2:1-4

The beggar who
could not walk
was healed through
Peter and John.

ACTS 3:1-10

Everyone shared
what they needed
and many were saved.
ACTS 2:42-47

Jesus appeared
one last time
and ascended
into heaven.

ACTS 1:6-11

# The Triumphal Entry

Jesus rode into Jerusalem on a donkey as a king in
what is known as "The Triumphal Entry."

---

*So they took branches of palm trees and went out to meet him, crying out, "Hosanna!
Blessed is he who comes in the name of the Lord, even the King of Israel!"*

JOHN 12:13

Before we jump into John 12, let's look back at John 11. Context is everything
and without chapter 11, chapter 12 would look very different.

*01* | In John 11, what miracle did Jesus perform?

Following this miracle, we find Jesus at dinner with Lazaraus and his sisters, Mary and Martha.

*02* | What did Mary do in John 12:3? What is the significance of this gesture?

According to Jewish custom, hosts washed the feet of their guests upon arrival. In this story, Mary goes above and beyond foot washing for Jesus. She modeled complete devotion. She took about a pint of pure nard, an expensive perfume, and poured it on Jesus' feet and wiped His feet with her hair. (John 12:3)

The social code of that day considered her actions scandalous. Why? Jewish women did not let their hair down in public because this expression of devotion was usually done behind closed doors and would have come across as extremely improper, even seductive.

We don't know why she chose to express her devotion this way. But, we do know that in making this gift ... by anointing Jesus with her precious oil ... she gave her very best ... all that she had.

Now that we've set the scene from John 11, let's study why Jesus chose to ride a donkey into Jerusalem.

*03* | **Read Zechariah 9:9. What does it say about Jesus?**

This is Jesus' grand entrance into the city. Yes, Jesus entered the world through a lowly birth, but now in John 12, we witness His triumphal entry. Many of those present were the same people who witnessed Jesus bring Lazarus back from the dead. They celebrated Jesus shouting, "Hosanna!" The Greek translation means "Oh save!" The crowd looked to Jesus as a political hero, a king who would rescue them from Roman oppression. But, what they would come to see is that He brought so much more than earthly leadership. In reality, this entrance was Jesus' inauguration into His role as King of kings. Jesus now rules as King in His heavenly Kingdom and continues to advance His Kingdom on earth every day as well. He is the Prince of Peace, the Holy One and the Savior of the World.

# The Last Supper and Betrayal

Jesus ate His last supper before being betrayed by Judas.

---

*I am not speaking of all of you; I know whom I have chosen. But the Scripture will be fulfilled, "He who ate my bread has lifted his heel against me."*

JOHN 13:18

Just before the Passover Feast, Jesus gathered His disciples to share a last meal together. His friends didn't know this would be their last supper with Him.

John 13 tells us Jesus knew His mission. He knew His identity. He knew where He was going. But, before He left, He had hard steps to walk through. First, Jesus knew the devil had prompted Judas to betray Him. He knew His disciples would scatter, and Peter would deny Him three times. He predicted these events. (John 13:21, 38; Matthew 26:31-34)

Even knowing these betrayals were coming, Jesus performed a most humble and precious act during the dinner. The King of kings and Lord of lords took the role of a servant. He gave His disciples a lesson in humility as He left the table, took off His outer clothes, wrapped a towel around His waist and washed their feet. An incredibly humble posture and act for their King and Messiah to perform.

After speaking a few more words, John tells us Jesus *"was troubled in his spirit, and testified, "Truly, truly, I say to you, one of you will betray me."*(John 13:21).

*01* | **Read Psalm 41:9. What does it say? What does the psalmist prophesy here?**

Read John 13:22-30 to see what happens after Jesus makes this prediction.

**02**     What did you think of the interaction between Peter and John? So like us, also, right? We want to be in the know. Who would betray their leader and teacher?

**03**     How did Jesus answer John's question in John 13:26? What happened in verse 27 when Jesus gave the bread to Judas?

I wonder if Jesus meant for that offer of bread to be a way out for Judas. To make him think about who Jesus was, about his friends, their mission and call. This moment is a beautiful example of how Jesus loves even His enemies.

But that didn't happen. Instead, we find four very hard words to read. "Satan entered into him" (John 13:27). Him being Judas.

**04**     Read John 13:27-30. What goes through your mind as you read Jesus' words to Judas to go quickly and do what he has committed to do?

Though it's heartbreaking to read and think about what Judas did, how Jesus' disciples scattered and how Peter would deny Him, it's comforting as well because Jesus knew what was coming. He knew His assignment.

God the Father sent God the Son to earth on a mission. (Genesis 3:15) Jesus knew He would be betrayed by one of His disciples to fulfill the God-ordained plan laid out for Jesus before time began. (Zechariah 11:12-13) He would be born of a virgin. (Isaiah 7:14) And then Jesus would live a life without sin, heal the sick, expose the law, be betrayed, crucified and resurrected. *This* was His purpose.

# Jesus' Trial and Crucifixion

Jesus was crucified on the cross.

*Then Jesus, calling out with a loud voice, said, "Father, into your hands I commit my spirit!"*
*And having said this he breathed his last.*

LUKE 23:46

Do you know what's crazy about today's study? While reading this passage of Scripture, I cried. My tears caught me off guard because I knew the third day was coming. I knew the glorious end to the story. I knew Jesus' death was not final. Yet, I still cried.

This day is hard to read because Jesus chose what He was about to endure. He chose to suffer an excruciating death. He chose to surround Himself with people who would betray and deny Him. And ultimately, He chose to die so we could live forever, free from sin and death, in eternity with Him.

God sent Jesus because He knew the longings we've been talking about reside in our hearts. He knew that one of those would be a longing for fulfillment. Jesus' death fulfilled a promise from God — His promise that He would never leave or forsake His people, no matter what. So, while the enemy may have felt victorious on that day, God knew Sunday was coming.

Friend, knowing Jesus' friends found the tomb empty on the third day gives us comfort for the tears we may cry today. Our God is a Promise Keeper.

01 | **Read Luke 23:1-25. Why do you think Pilate sent Jesus to Herod, and then Herod sent Jesus back to Pilate? How many times did Pilate try to release Jesus? (Luke 23:22)**

Pilate, Rome's governing leader during this time, had a reputation of being a cruel man. And, yet, Pilate found no wrong in Jesus. That says something, doesn't it?

I struggle with Pilate's story personally. Maybe you do too. I can be quite the people-pleaser. However, when it comes to my convictions or my faith in Jesus, I'd like to believe I wouldn't give into my people-pleasing nature.

*02*    **Read Matthew 27:24. If Pilate believed Jesus to be innocent, why do you think he still went through with crucifying Jesus?**

In the midst of what's happening, we meet a man named Barabbas. You can find his story in Matthew 27:15-26. Who is this man? Scripture identifies him as an insurrectionist and a murderer. Maybe among the worst of sinners at that time. A sinner like us. A sinner in need of a Savior.

Barabbas' story makes this passage a bit more personal, doesn't it? Barabbas, a criminal, released from prison, lived, while Jesus, the Son of God, took his place and died. You and me, sinners freed from sin and death, live, while Jesus, the Son of God, took our place, dying the death we deserved. How thankful I am for Jesus' grace. Barabbas, a murderer. You and me, sinners. Jesus, sinless. The grace of the Lord knows no bounds for His children.

*03*    **Read Jesus' final words from Matthew 27:46. Can you remember a time when this has been a desperate cry of your heart? Romans 8:28 tells us God is working all things together for good for those who love Him and are called according to His purpose. Even places as hard as an innocent man dying on a cross. How can you see God working in the hurting places in your past or present?**

Matthew 27:50 tells us Jesus cried out and yielded up His spirit. Pay attention to these words. No one took Jesus' life from Him. Death had no hold on the sinless Son of God. No, He chose to die. He chose to stand in our place, though undeserving, perfect and sinless in every way.

Jesus fulfilled the words of the prophet Isaiah written thousands of years earlier. Jesus, despised and rejected by men, carried our sorrows. He was pierced for our transgressions, crushed for our iniquities. (Isaiah 53:3-5) Yet, by some incredible miracle, by His wounds we are healed.

Jesus' suffering and death fulfilled our every longing — especially our longing to be loved and valued for all eternity. God the Father tore the veil that had separated Him from His people since the Fall. Jesus' sacrificial love for us opened the way for us to be in relationship with God the Father and commune with Him anytime, anywhere.

# unlikely mercies

| TRIAL/ HARDSHIP | WHERE WE FIND THE STORYLINE | UNLIKELY MERCY/ BLESSING/GOOD |
|---|---|---|
| Adam and Eve ejected from the Garden of Eden and separated from God | GENESIS 3:8-24 | Spared from eating from the Tree of Life and from perpetual separation from God |
| Hagar in the wilderness | GENESIS 21:8-21 | God came and called her by name and promised her that her son would be the father of many nations |
| Joseph's wrongful imprisonment | GENESIS 39:19-21 | What man meant for evil God used to be great provision for Joseph, his family, Egypt and surrounding nations |
| Israelites enslaved in Egypt | JOSHUA 5:2-12 | The Israelites strengthened in numbers |
| David hunted by Saul and wandering in the wilderness | 1 SAMUEL 23:14 | God protected David and prepared him for his role as king, strengthening, humbling and teaching him how to lead people |
| The cross | MARK 15:12-24; JOHN 3:16 | Salvation and eternal life |

# The Resurrection

Jesus walked and ate with His disciples.

---

*"While they were talking and discussing together, Jesus himself drew near and went with them."*
LUKE 24:15

## He is not here,
## but has risen.

### LUKE 24:6

Oh friend, what a day to rejoice and celebrate! The Savior of the world did not stay in the grave. He rose from the dead.

Luke 24:4 tells us the women who went to see Jesus were perplexed when they found no body. Even though Jesus prophesied His death, they did not expect to find an empty tomb.

*01* | **Can you think of a time Jesus has resurrected a dream, relationship or healed something/ someone you thought was beyond repair?**

Luke's Gospel tells us the women returned to the 11 disciples and shared the news of the empty tomb. The men did not believe them. Peter and John ran to the tomb to see for themselves.

*02* | **Sitting on this side of the resurrection story, who do you relate to in this story? The women going to care for Jesus' body? Peter and John running to the tomb? Or the disciples who remained behind? Why?**

John 20:9 says, *"for as yet they did not understand the Scripture, that he must rise from the dead."* Even after walking with Jesus throughout His ministry, hearing Him prophesy His death and seeing the empty tomb, Peter still marveled at what had happened. (Luke 24:12)

Jesus didn't stay hidden after His resurrection. We see Him on the road to Emmaus in Luke 24, drawing near to two of His followers (Cleopas and an unnamed man), joining them on their walk from Jerusalem to Emmaus. Luke tells us they *"were kept from recognizing him,"* (Luke 24:16) despite walking and talking with Him for several miles. In fact, they unknowingly explained to Jesus who He was and who they thought He was going to be!

Jesus walked patiently with them, listening, until they arrived in Emmaus. In Luke 24:28-34, while sharing a meal with them, Jesus finally opened their eyes and revealed His identity. The two men immediately got up, returned to Jerusalem, and told the disciples how they had seen the risen Jesus!

In Luke 24:36, while Cleopas and his friend shared their story, Jesus Himself appeared among them. Sensing their fear, Jesus spoke these words, *"Peace to you."* Then, He ate with them, just as He had done countless times before. Afterward, He explained, again, how His death and resurrection fulfilled the law (given by Moses), the prophets and the Psalms. Those three words (law, prophets and psalms) covered the entire Old Testament from beginning to end. Jesus was ensuring His followers knew He fulfilled everything the Old Testament spoke of.

I love Jesus' next words. In Luke 24:45, it says, *"Then [Jesus] opened their minds to understand the Scriptures."* He gave them understanding, wisdom, knowledge and discernment.

The same is true for us. We have God's infallible Word within our reach. Jesus' death, resurrection and ascension to heaven made this possible. His death tore the veil so we can go straight to God the Father with our questions. His resurrection made it possible for us to be raised up with Jesus spiritually, sitting with Him at the right hand of God, with Him interceding on our behalf. (Ephesians 2:6; Colossians 3:1; Romans 8:34) And, Jesus' ascension gave us the gift of God the Holy Spirit to know and understand God and His Word better and deeper. (John 16:7)

# The Holy Spirit is Given

The Holy Spirit came as promised, to dwell inside
all believers and establish union in Christ.

---

*"When the day of Pentecost arrived, they were all together in one place. And suddenly there came from heaven
a sound like a mighty rushing wind, and it filled the entire house where they were sitting. And divided tongues
as of fire appeared to them and rested on each one of them. And they were all filled with the Holy Spirit and
began to speak in other tongues as the Spirit gave them utterance."*

ACTS 2:1-4

*01*　Read Acts 2:1-4. Describe in your own words what you read.

Jesus' last words before He ascended into heaven must have sounded strange to the disciples: *"But you will receive
power when the Holy Spirit has come upon you, and you will be my witnesses in Jerusalem and in all Judea and Samaria,
and to the ends of the earth"* (Acts 1:8). I wonder if they remembered Jesus had spoken similar words to them before.
We find them in John's Gospel.

*02*　Take a few minutes to read John 14 (focus on verses 25-26). What did Jesus say would
happen? Who would send the Holy Spirit? How does Jesus describe the Holy Spirit?

I love how our God is a promise keeper! He promised to send the Holy Spirit and on the day of Pentecost, God
honored His Word. He sent His promised gift.

Pentecost is a Greek word meaning "50." Pentecost fell on the 50th day after Passover — the Jewish festival where
the people brought the first fruits of their wheat harvest to God. (Exodus 34:22-23)

As the people gathered in Jerusalem, they saw and experienced three strange and marvelous events. First and suddenly, *"... there came from heaven a sound like a mighty rushing wind, and it filled the entire house where they were sitting"* (Acts 2:2). Second, *"divided tongues as of fire appeared to them and rested on each one of them"* (Acts 2:3).

*03* | **We find baptism present with fire somewhere else in the New Testament. Read Matthew 3:11. What does it say?**

And, finally the most miraculous moment of all, God filled the men from Galilee with His Holy Spirit, enabling them to speak in foreign tongues they had never learned. Galileans were looked upon as uneducated, uncultured and poor speakers, so this was truly astounding to those listening.

People from surrounding areas, who spoke different languages, came to see what was happening and also stood amazed as they heard these Galilean men speaking in their individual native tongues as the Holy Spirit enabled them.

The Holy Spirit came and rested on these men individually to unite them in a new way, a way that had never been done before in the history of God's people. He united them as one, through the power of His Holy Spirit, to be members of His Body, to usher in the beginning of His Church. God's intent was to build his Church from Jews and Gentiles, cultured and uncultured, wise and not so wise. A multi-racial and multicultural Church.

*04* | **What did the ones speaking in tongues declare? (Acts 2:11)**

The disciples thanked God and praised Him in unknown tongues. The gathered crowd *overheard* what the disciples declared to God, each in their own language.

And then, Peter, our most beloved Peter, stood before everyone gathered in that place and proclaimed the gospel with a boldness, confidence and courage we've not seen before. He'd come a long way since the Peter who denied knowing Christ.

Peter confronted the Jews with the truth about themselves and about Jesus. He used Old Testament Scripture to teach them salvation comes not by obeying the law but by faith alone. He explained Jesus was the Messiah for whom they were waiting. He confronted them with their sin of denying, persecuting and killing Jesus. He proclaimed the truth about how Jesus fulfilled the Old Testament and fulfilled the words Jesus Himself prophesied. Jesus rose from the dead and is seated at the right hand of God. He has now poured out His Holy Spirit on His people. He told them the time had now come for them to repent and be baptized for the forgiveness of sins so they too could receive the gift of the Holy Spirit.

Peter called them to turn toward God and away from the things that are not of God. He told them to be baptized in the name of Jesus.

*05* | **Read Acts 2:37-41. How did Peter's words affect the crowd? What did they ask? How did Peter respond?**

Through Peter's words, and the working power of the Holy Spirit, more than 3,000 people came to Christ that day! (Acts 2:41)

*06* | **Read Acts 2:42-47. What did the new believers do and how did they live?**

These believers came together as ONE! They learned the Word together. They shared all they had. They served one another. They broke bread together. They helped those in need. They lived layered lives together. And, God made Himself evident by performing miraculous wonders in their midst.

*07* | **Are you in community with other believers? What does that look like? Do you see God at work in your midst? If you haven't yet found community, pray for God to open a door for you to join with other believers.**

God the Father is a Promise Keeper. God the Son is a Promise Keeper. God the Holy Spirit is a Promise Keeper. While I may not always remember those attributes of God, I know without a doubt He is there and with me.

This week, we experienced a roller coaster of emotions. We witnessed Jesus, the Son of Man and Savior of the world, receive praise and adoration from the masses as He rode into Jerusalem. We witnessed His excruciating betrayal, denial and death. Yet, what appeared to be a tragic and final ending on the cross became a beautiful backdrop for Jesus' glorious and triumphant return.

Remember what Jesus shared with His disciples before He ascended to heaven? *"Everything written about me in the Law of Moses and the Prophets and the Psalms must be fulfilled"* (Luke 24:44). Jesus would suffer on the cross; He would resurrect on the third day, and He would ascend into heaven. But, it all had purpose. Jesus suffered through it all so that salvation could be proclaimed and forgiveness and new life given to all people and nations.

After Jesus' resurrection and ascension, we walked with Luke in the early chapters of Acts through the step-by-step establishment and expansion of the New Testament church. We watched with amazement as Jesus poured out His Holy Spirit onto His people, equipping and empowering them to take the gospel to the ends of the earth, just as Jesus commanded them at the end of Matthew 28 — often referred to as the Great Commission.

But, the Holy Spirit's work didn't stop with Acts. God the Father continues to pour God the Spirit out on His people today. Believers have the Spirit of the Living God indwelling, empowering and equipping them to take that same gospel to our corner of the world — to the people and places He is leading and directing us.

# Jesus, thank You for dying on the cross for my sins.

Thank You for defeating death and raising from the grave on the third day. God the Father, thank You for paying the ultimate price in sending Your Son to die an excruciating death so that I may have life with You. Today, I pray for a renewed strength to be bold in my faith, as Jesus modeled. Lord, thank You for forgiving me of my sins and for sending Your Holy Spirit to dwell within me. Thank You for giving me Your Word to learn from, to tattoo on my heart and to share with my neighbor. God, You are merciful, gracious and so good. I pray I never take for granted having a personal relationship with You. Bless my path and fill me with Your Holy Spirit. We ask all of this in Jesus' name. Amen.

# longing

# for ———————— *week seven*

# identity

# One of the first things you would recognize about me is that I'm Indian. My cultural and ethnic background has always been a special aspect of who I am.

For instance, I love when someone comes up to me and shares their love for Indian food! However, growing up, my ethnic background had me asking some specific questions. *Who am I? How does my Indian heritage impact my life living in the United States?* Ultimately, I found myself questioning my identity. This is something we likely all question regardless of our ethnic, social or cultural background. At some point in time, or maybe at many points in time, we've asked "Who am I?"

There is really good news for us! God's Word gives us this answer in the most clear and concise manner. Genesis 1:26-28 says,
*"Then God said, 'Let us make man in our image, after our likeness. And let them have dominion over the fish of the sea and over the birds of the heavens and over the livestock and over all the earth and over every creeping thing that creeps on the earth.' So God created man in his own image, in the image of God he created him; male and female he created them. And God blessed them. And God said to them, 'Be fruitful and multiply and fill the earth and subdue it, and have dominion over the fish of the sea and over the birds of the heavens and over every living thing that moves on the earth.'"*

When 20th-century theologian Dietrich von Hildebrand of Germany saw the travesty and tragedy of Hitler's murderous actions against those of Jewish descent, he said, "All of Western Christian civilization stands and falls with the words of Genesis, God made man in His image."

I would suggest we can remove "Western Christian" and just say "all of humanity." Hildebrand saw within Scripture the dignity of all mankind as image bearers of God.

Genesis reminds us that our identity is wrapped up in the will and wisdom of God who created us equal in value and worth, and yet distinct and diverse. God defines us not by what we do, but by whose we are. Sadly, after the Fall, the longing for identity turned us inward, looking to ourselves for our meaning, value and worth. Henri Nouwen, whose work as a priest and professor focused on psychology, social justice and community, warns us of five lies of identity:

1) I am what I have.
2) I am what I do.
3) I am what other people say or think of me.
4) I am nothing more than my worst moment.
5) I am nothing less than my best moment.

As we look at Scripture, I have a suspicion that Stephen, Saul (who would become Paul) and Peter all faced aspects of these lies about their identity:

Stephen, the first Christian martyr, may have been caught in an "I am what I do" moment where he knew what he did and how he spoke would be a reflection of his beliefs. (Acts 7) Saul may have been tormented by "I am nothing more than my worst moment" thoughts since he was the instigator and initiator of Stephen's murder. (Acts 7:57-Acts 8:1)

Peter may have been horrified by his impulse to compromise for the sake of what others thought of him in an "I am what other people say or think of me" moment. (Luke 22:54-62)

However, for each of these lies, there is a brilliant truth.

1. My identity is what I have in Christ – salvation and freedom from sin and death.

2. I don't have to worry about "doing" because Christ has done all that was needed to be done on the cross.

3. I am what God says of me, and that is the only thing that matters.

4. My relationship with God is safe and secure even in the midst of my very worst moments.

5. I rejoice in all that God has done for me in my very best moments.

This whole time, we have been talking about our individual identity. But the lives of Stephen, Paul and Peter all point to the interconnected reality of our personal life with the lives of others. Our identity is not simply about us; it is about our relationship with God Who rewrites our story into His story. Our new story is to be lived out in order to invite others into the beautiful story of God who makes all things new and restores beauty from chaos.

Who are we? We are image bearers of God.

Whose are we? We belong wholly and fully to God the Father.

What are we supposed to do? We are to spread the glory of God to the ends of the earth by making disciples of Jesus amongst all the nations. (Matthew 28:16-20)

# This is our identity.

Jesus appeared to Saul and ordered him to preach the good news of Jesus to all.
ACTS 9:1-19

After being persecuted, Saul escaped from Damascus to Jerusalem.
ACTS 9:23-25

Peter began his ministry.
ACTS 9:32-11:18

Stephen was the first person recorded to give his life for speaking the good news of Jesus.
ACTS 7:60

Saul persecuted the Church.
ACTS 8:1-3

Saul proclaimed the good news of Jesus.
ACTS 9:20-22

Barnabas brought Paul to the disciples.
ACTS 9:26-31

The Holy Spirit was poured out while Peter was preaching.

ACTS 10:45

By the power of God, Peter spoke to a dead woman named Dorcas and told her to arise.

ACTS 9:36-43

Peter was rescued from prison by an angel of the Lord who appeared in his cell.

ACTS 12:6-19

Peter is given a vision to extend God's grace to all non-Jews (gentiles).

ACTS 10:1-43

Herod was struck dead and eaten by worms immediately after he was praised as having *"the voice of a god and not of a man"* and did not deny it.

ACTS 12:20-25

By the power of God, Peter commanded a man named Aeneas, bedridden for eight years, to walk again.

ACTS 9:32-35

James, the brother of John, was killed, and Peter was imprisoned for simply belonging to the Church.

ACTS 12:1-5

Paul preached to
the entire city of
Antioch in Pisidia.
ACTS 13:13-52

Paul and Barnabas
set out on what has
been called the First
Missionary Journey.
ACTS 13:2-3;
ACTS 13-14

In Lystra, Paul was worshiped
by some as a god for the
miracles that followed him,
and He was beaten with stones
by Jews from Antioch and Iconium.
ACTS 14:8-23

Saul
is
now
called
Paul.
ACTS 13:9

Paul and Barnabas spoke at
the city of Iconium in Galatia
and a large number of both
Jews and Greeks believed.
ACTS 14:1-7

Paul and Barnabas
returned to their
home base in Antioch
in Syria before starting
the next journey.
ACTS 14:24-28

# Stephen is Martyred

Stephen was the first person recorded to give his life
for speaking the good news of Jesus.

---

*And falling to his knees he cried out with a loud voice, "Lord, do not
hold this sin against them." And when he had said this, he fell asleep.*

ACTS 7:60

Before we jump into our main verse for today, let's summarize what has just happened. In Acts 6, the 12 apostles chose a man named Stephen to be one of seven men to carry out practical and administrative duties.

## List and pay careful attention to the words used to describe Stephen. (Acts 6:3, 5, 8)

Luke tells us opposition arose against those who professed and publicly shared Jesus as their Lord and Savior. As these men argued and debated with Stephen, Acts 6:10 says, *"… they could not withstand the wisdom and the Spirit with which he was speaking."*

Driven by fear, anger and hatred, they seized Stephen and brought false charges against him. Even before the trial began, Scripture tells us Stephen's face *"was like the face of an angel"* (Acts 6:15). Did they really see an "angelic" face like the ones we see in paintings and drawings? I don't think so. I believe what they saw was an overflow of the One who indwelled Stephen. Stephen's face reflected a peace … a confidence … in the God He loved and in Whom He trusted. God's presence had been with him and in him and was rising up in its fullness as he prepared to fight and contend for God and His people.

*01* Who else experienced this kind of overflow of God's Spirit? Read Exodus 34:29-35. Share what these two stories speak to you about the realities of the Spirit of the Living God living within us and how it influences our everyday living.

In response to the charges brought against him, Stephen did not defend himself. Instead, in the longest speech in Acts, Stephen brought charges against his accusers. He called these New Testament Jews *"stiff-necked people, uncircumcised in heart and ears,"* (Acts 7:51) who followed in the footsteps of their forefathers who repeatedly hardened their hearts, stiffened their necks and closed their ears to the work of God.

Stephen's words infuriated his accusers so much that Acts 7:56 says, *"they gnashed their teeth at him."*

What comes next is beautiful! A supernatural moment happens in the midst of Stephen's persecution. Luke describes this moment in Acts 7:55, *"Stephen, filled through all his being with the Holy Spirit, looked steadily up into Heaven"* (JB Phillips' translation). Filled through all his being! Oh, friend, when we trust in Jesus, we have that very same Spirit living in us. Let us pursue Jesus so deeply, engage with Him so intimately that we too can be filled so full that God's Spirit saturates us from head to toe.

*02* | **Read Acts 7:56. What did Stephen see?**

Did you notice something unique about Stephen's vision? Most often we hear of Jesus sitting at His Father's right hand. But, here, Stephen saw Jesus *standing* at His right hand. This brings tears to my eyes. I can't help but think Jesus is giving Stephen a standing ovation. Honoring him in the last moments of his life. Giving Stephen assurance that He understands because He had been where Stephen was. Despised. Rejected. Falsely accused. Unjustly persecuted.

*03* | **Read Acts 7:57-58. Who stood close by watching Stephen's stoning?**

Luke closes this chapter with the last moments of Stephen's life. While they were stoning him, Stephen prayed, *"Lord Jesus, receive my spirit."* Then Stephen fell on his knees and cried out, *"Lord, do not hold this sin against them"* (Acts 7:59-60). Words that take us back to Jesus on the cross, when Jesus also spoke similar words of forgiveness, *"Father, forgive them, for they know not what they do"* (Luke 23:34).

We know God answered Stephen's last prayer of forgiveness. Because Saul, who stood near and watched Stephen's stoning, soon encountered Jesus in a personal and powerful way that forever transformed his heart. St. Augustine concluded we owe the conversion of Saul to the prayers of Stephen.

Friend, may we be like Stephen. May we be God's vessel, as Stephen was to Paul, to transform the hearts of those who don't believe. To draw them closer to His Word, His heart and His Kingdom purposes for their lives.

*04* | **Write a prayer asking God the Spirit to fill you with all His fullness and invade every part of your being. Invite Him to bring you supernatural experiences exceedingly abundantly above what you could ever ask or imagine. Appeal to Him to open doors for you to bring truth, hope and healing into this hurting world.**

## Oh, Lord, as we leave today, will you show us Your Glory?
# Lord, show us Your glory!

# Saul

## Saul Persecuted the Church.

---

*"But Saul was ravaging the church, and entering house after house,*
*he dragged off men and women and committed them to prison."*

ACTS 8:3

Stephen's stoning incited widespread persecution against the church. Saul led the way *"ravaging the church"* (Acts 8:3, NASB), forcefully entering believers' houses, mistreating them and dragging them off to prison. (Acts 8:1) We can only imagine the terror that filled believers' hearts as they watched and experienced Saul's brazen acts of cruelty.

Yet, rather than run and hide from their persecutors, the persecuted ones grew stronger and bolder. Luke tells us they "scattered" throughout Judea and Samaria, preaching the gospel wherever their feet carried them. (Acts 8:4) The word "scatter" derives from the Greek word *diaspeiro*, which means "to sow throughout, to disperse like a seed." How I love this image! These persecuted believers, in the midst of being hunted like animals, went out sowing seeds of truth, love and hope.

01 | **Read Acts 1:8. How were these believers living and obeying this command? Why do you think they hadn't done that until now?**

Sometimes God uses our hardest, most trying circumstances to lead us to His assignments. Sometimes He shakes us up to take us out of our comfort zones and into His perfect will. We can trust that nothing we live through is wasted in the hands of our Almighty God. No matter how unforeseen, unfortunate or tragic. It's all in the lens through which we view our circumstance. Will we view it with a willing heart to look beyond the hurt, pain and doubt and find the Romans 8:28 good God promises for His children ... for those who love Him and are called according to His purpose?

Remember, these early believers were not professional teachers and preachers. Most were everyday people like you and me. People who had a story to tell. A message to share about the One who had saved and transformed their lives. And God still uses His children today to draw people to Jesus. Yes, some are pastors and preachers. But sometimes, God chooses people like you and me to share the hope we've found. People with whom those listening can identify and relate. People who live what they believe as best they can. People who love, care and pray for others. People who invest in them.

*02* Will you join me in stepping out in faith today to touch the life of another? Prayerfully open your Bible at the end of this lesson. Ask God to give you a "word" for a friend, family member or even stranger. Ask God, "who is this for?" Invite Him to lead you to that person. Ask Him how to share what you found. You may notice and encourage someone you normally wouldn't see. You may bring hope where there's despair. Love where there's an empty ache. Peace where there's extreme anxiety. Trust God with this assignment, friend. El Roi, the God who sees, will be faithful.

God also used Stephen's persecution to raise up an evangelist. God's first evangelist. His name is Philip. We read about him, and his interaction with the Ethiopian eunuch, earlier. Philip was one of the seven, like Stephen, chosen to help the apostles with administrative duties. But, after Stephen's death, God changed the trajectory of Philip's life. Philip chose to go where no Jews would ever go, Samaria, to minister to the people there.

*03* Read John 4:9. What does it say about the relationship between Jews and Samaritans?

The Samaritans were half-Jew, half-gentile. The Jews hated the gentiles, even the God-fearing ones, because they stopped short of becoming full Jews in lifestyle and in circumcision. They considered gentiles unclean and refused to associate with them, open their homes to them or share meals with them.

This mixed-race came about after the Assyrians took over the northern kingdom of Israel in 721 B.C. Some of the Jews stayed behind and intermarried with the Assyrians, producing the Samaritans.

Oh friend, sometimes the people the hardest to love are not those on the other side of the world but those closest to us, whose skin color, culture, history and customs are different from ours. Yet, Phillip chose to go to these people. To the people the Jews refused and rejected. He invested his heart and time in them. He shared the gospel and performed miracles that led many of them to Christ, expanding the church geographically and culturally.

It pains my heart to think of the rejection, persecution and annihilation the Jews have endured through the centuries. All because of where they live and the genes they carry. God's Word commands us to love all people because we all bear the image of God. This is what God later revealed to Peter in a dream. Our identity is not determined by the nation from which we originate, the color of our skin, or what others say or think of us. Our identity is found in Christ alone and what He did for us on the cross. It's found in what God says of us ... we are loved, forgiven, saved, redeemed, valued, created with great intention and purpose. I'm so thankful for Philip's story and want it to be my story, our story. To love and scatter seeds to *all* people God brings across our paths.

*04* | **Who is in your sphere of influence? Who can you walk alongside and share your story and your faith. What uncomfortable space can you step into to scatter your seed? Write down that person's name. Pray and ask God how you can lead them closer to Jesus. And, if a name doesn't come to mind, pray for one. God will be faithful!**

Philip continued to play a vital role in the expansion of God's Kingdom. Huge crowds gathered to hear him and many put their faith in Jesus.

# Saul's Conversion

Jesus appeared to Saul and ordered him to preach the good news of Jesus to all.

---

*And falling to the ground, he heard a voice saying to him, "Saul, Saul, why are you persecuting me?"*

ACTS 9:4

Today we encounter Saul, a man who experienced one of the most profound heart transformations in all of Scripture. The man who ruthlessly ravaged and persecuted the Lord's beloved sons and daughters becomes God's greatest preacher and advocate.

At one point, Saul, filled with hatred and a zealousness to protect his Jewish heritage, sought official permission to pursue the believers who had escaped to Damascus after Stephen's death and bring them back to Jerusalem to imprison them. If you want to read more of what Paul has to say personally about his background, read Philippians 3:1-10 and Galatians 1:13-17.

But God! Don't you love those words? God interrupted Saul's plans because He had greater plans in store for him. While on the road to Damascus, Saul witnessed a light from heaven flash about him. A light so brilliant and powerful he fell to the ground. In that moment, he heard a voice, *"Saul, Saul why are you persecuting me?"* (Acts 9:4) The men with him stood speechless, hearing nothing but seeing its effects.

*01* | Reread Acts 9:4. Who was Saul persecuting? How do you think those words impacted Saul? **The God he thought he was so vigorously and viciously defending was actually the very one he was fighting.**

Saul asked who was speaking to him. The Voice replied, *"I am Jesus, whom you are persecuting"* (Acts 9:5). Jesus instructed Saul to get up and head into the city for more instructions.

As Saul got up to leave, he realized he was blind. For the next three days, Saul remained unable to see and did not eat or drink. The Lord put him in a place where he was dying to self. Letting go of what drove him for years. His heritage. His name. His identity. His reputation. His intelligence. All brought low compared to the glory of his God.

Can you imagine Saul's emotions during that encounter? The One whom he alleged was dead and powerless. The One whose followers he had been imprisoning and persecuting left the splendor of heaven to make Himself known to Saul.

What a glorious and intimate encounter! Saul met the living Christ that day.

*02* | **Read Matthew 23:12. How does this verse come into play?**

Saul obeyed Jesus' instructions and went into the city to find a disciple and believer in Jesus named Ananias. The Lord had gone before Saul and given Ananias instructions as well. He warned him that Saul was coming. God instructed Ananias in a vision to go to Saul and restore his sight.

*03* | **Read Acts 9:10-16. What specific instructions did the Lord give to Ananias? How did Ananias, who was a believer, respond to the Lord's request? What did God say to comfort Ananias? What was Saul's assignment from the Lord?**

We know Ananias trusted the Lord's words because in Acts 9:17, Ananias goes to Saul.

*04* | How does Ananias address Saul in verse 17?

I find this so powerful. He believed the Lord's words so deeply that he called this persecutor of God's people "brother." Oh, that I would be so quick to respond when the Lord calls me to reconcile, ask forgiveness, be kind when everything in me says no because they don't deserve it.

*05* | How does Ananias' response to Saul encourage and equip you for the next time you face a challenge like this?

Ananias had a heart conversion as well. Trust and love replaced distrust and fear. He came to see Saul as a brother rather than an enemy.

# Peter

### Peter began his ministry.

---

*"If then God gave the same gift to them as he gave to us when we believed in the Lord Jesus Christ, who was I that I could stand in God's way?" When they heard these things they fell silent. And they glorified God, saying, "Then to the Gentiles also God has granted repentance that leads to life."*

ACTS 11:17-18

Acts 11 commemorates a momentous event in the history of the Christian Church. God used Peter, one of Jesus' beloved 12, to change the landscape of the Christian Church forever.

The account begins in Acts 10 where we meet an important God-fearing man in the Roman army named Cornelius. Essential to our story is the fact he was a gentile, a non-Jew by birth.

God spoke to Cornelius in a dream, telling him to send men to Joppa to find Peter the apostle and invite him to Cornelius' home in Caesarea. Cornelius obeyed and sent his men to Peter.

At the same time, Peter received a vision from God in which a voice instructed him to kill and eat animals lowered from heaven on a white sheet. The problem was some of the animals were unclean. Old Testament law forbade God's people to eat unclean animals. So Peter refused, *"By no means, Lord, for I have never eaten anything common or unclean"* (Acts 10:14).

The voice spoke a second time, speaking faith-rocking, church-transforming words to Peter, *"What God has made clean, do not call common"* (Acts 10:15).

*01* | Read Acts 10:9-16. Why do you think God gave Peter this vision three times?

Cornelius' request asked Peter to set aside long-standing laws and traditions. And, isn't that why Jesus came? To fulfill the law? To bring freedom? To break down barriers? For more insight, read Matthew 5:17-18, Acts 13:38-39 and Romans 8:3-4;10:4.

Peter accepted Cornelius' scandalous invitation, taking six believing brothers with him. In doing so, he broke every Jewish social restriction of the time.

When Peter heard Cornelius' explanation of why he had sent for him, everything became clear. Peter understood the life-saving, faith-transforming message of Jesus was for everyone! God's vision made clear from that point forward, *all* who believe in Jesus and receive forgiveness of sins through His name will be saved. (Acts 10:34-35)

As Peter shared the gospel, the Holy Spirit fell upon those listening, just as He had done at Pentecost. (Acts 2:4) Peter spoke ground-breaking words to those present, *"'Can anyone withhold water for baptizing these people, who have received the Holy Spirit just as we have?' And he commanded them to be baptized in the name of Jesus Christ ..."* (Acts 10:47-48).

02 | **Read Acts 2:1-13 to understand the significance the Holy Spirit coming upon them must have held to Peter and those with him.**

Upon Peter's return to Jerusalem, the circumcised believers criticized him for associating and sharing a meal with gentiles. Peter, prepared for their words of judgment, did not defend himself. Instead, he presented a case to the men accusing him. A fact-filled, witness-driven case defending God, not Peter.

First, Peter brought forth the six men who had accompanied him to be witnesses to the words he was about to speak. Second, Peter relayed the entire story, beginning with Cornelius' dream and how he sent the men to Peter. Peter then shared his vision in vivid detail. He specifically shared how he came to understand that the vision of the unclean animals had to do with people and not food.

Third, he shared how the Holy Spirit fell upon Cornelius and his household just as it had fallen upon all of them at Pentecost.

*03* Read Acts 11:16-17. What justification did Peter give for believing as he did, and whose words did he quote? Here are a few more verses to support Peter's decision: Genesis 12:3; 22:18; Ephesians 3:1-6.

*04* Read Acts 11:18. How did the circumcised believers respond?

The tender-hearted, faithful obedience of Cornelius and Peter ushered in a new era for the church. For the first time, missionaries intentionally reached out to share the gospel with gentiles. What began with Philip in Samaria and with Peter in Caesarea grew into a movement that started the church in Antioch. It was here that two unnamed missionaries brought great numbers of people to Jesus.

Just as God did with Peter, He often has to change our thinking so we can be better instruments of His faith-generating, life-transforming message. God is most glorified when the church reflects the Kingdom — when it reflects His mosaic culturally, racially and socially. Beloved sons and daughters who might never walk together in life come together to be the Church because of the love and saving grace of Jesus.

# The First Missionary Journey

Paul and Barnabas set out on what has been called the First Missionary Journey.

---

*While they were worshiping the Lord and fasting, the Holy Spirit said, "Set apart for me Barnabas and Saul for the work to which I have called them." Then after fasting and praying they laid their hands on them and sent them off.*

ACTS 13:2-3

Today's reading leads us into a busy and exciting time for the early Church. The mission work that began with Philip and Peter exploded into prayerful, intentional mission work led by people called and committed to live out Jesus' last words: *"Go therefore and make disciples of all nations"* and *"be my witnesses in Jerusalem and in all Judea and Samaria, and to the ends of the earth"* (Matthew 28:19; Acts 1:8).

The church at Antioch, the first truly multi-ethnic local church, became a mighty tool in this missionary era, equipping and sending out missionaries who created

multitudes of disciples. Why this church? Because its leaders regularly led the people in the study of God's Word. They also faithfully fasted, prayed and actively sought to hear from God.

Acts 13 opens with the Holy Spirit speaking and instructing those fasting and praying to, *"Set apart for me Barnabas and Saul (who for the first time in this chapter will also be called Paul, his Roman name] for the work to which I have called them"* (Acts 13:2). The leaders obeyed, laid hands on Barnabas and Paul and sent them out.

*01* Read Acts 9:15-16, where God identifies Paul's call. Read Ephesians 2:10, words later written by Paul. How do these verses relate to what was happening to Paul at this time? How do they speak to you where you are in your life?

These two men, at times accompanied by a man named John Mark (who later wrote the gospel of Mark), served as a dynamic duo as they traveled from city to city boldly and clearly proclaiming salvation. Along the way, they experienced great success but also endured great persecution. No matter what they encountered, though, they never gave up.

Their third stop took them to Paphos, a spiritually dark city famous for its worship of Venus, the goddess of sexual love. Amazingly, the proconsul or governor of the island, described as a "man of intelligence," came to hear them speak. In the midst of their preaching, a magician and Jewish false prophet, seeking to turn the proconsul away from the faith, interrupted them, making a nuisance of himself. Let's read what happened next:

*... Paul, filled with the Holy Spirit, looked intently at him and said, "You son of the devil, you enemy of all righteousness, full of all deceit and villainy, will you not stop making crooked the straight paths of the Lord? And now, behold, the hand of the Lord is upon you, and you will be blind and unable to see the sun for a time." Immediately mist and darkness fell upon him, and he went about seeking people to lead him by the hand. Then the proconsul believed, when he saw what had occurred, for he was astonished at the teaching of the Lord.* (Acts 13:9-12)

*02* | **What stood out to you as Paul addressed this false prophet named Bar-Jesus. What physically happened to Bar-Jesus? What does this remind you of from our lesson in Day 3? (Acts 9)**

*03* | **How did the proconsul respond?**

What a beautiful story of conversion. I don't think it was the miracle of inflicting blindness that impressed and astonished the proconsul as much as Paul's teaching and his boldness, conviction and courage to contend for what he believed.

In each city along the way, Barnabas and Saul taught in the synagogues. They opened in prayer, read from the Torah and preached the prophets. Paul consistently taught that everything in Israel's history led, and pointed, to the coming of Jesus and salvation for sinners through His death and resurrection. Paul's heart was for people to know that God had a plan for history before time began and all people from Abraham's time, to Paul's time, to our time are in the flow of that plan. To know God is greater than man's sin and rebellion, and Jesus rose in triumph over sin and death.

Each time cities expelled Paul and Barnabas, they shook the dust from their feet and moved on, filled with joy and the Holy Spirit. (Matthew 10:14) Great multitudes, both Jews and gentiles, came to believe!

As they closed out this first missionary journey, they revisited the cities in which they had been to strengthen those who were saved and exhort them to stand firm in the faith. They established new churches and made disciples all along the way!

God's methodology hasn't changed, friend. God continues His mission of sending, pursuing, seeking and saving today. Desiring not one be lost. (2 Peter 3:9) God invites us, His beloved sons and daughters, to join Him on this mission.

04 | **Read Romans 10:17. Write this verse in your own words and write what it means to you. How can you participate in making this verse come true in the life of another?**

Friend, God's Word is like a seed. We are the vessels God uses to scatter His seed. Once scattered, the Lord watches over it to ensure it takes root, grows and produces abundant fruit. Let's go scatter some seeds today!

# What an incredible week we've had watching God's church grow from a small band of Jewish Jesus followers to an emboldened army of evangelists.

This transformational journey began with Stephen's bold, brave, Spirit-filled sermon that led to his unjust death that incited widespread persecution.

But, rather than give in to their fear, the persecuted ones grew stronger and bolder. Luke tells us they "scattered" throughout Judea and Samaria. These persecuted believers, in the midst of being hunted like animals, went out sowing seeds of truth, love and hope.

The brightest light during this time came when God turned Saul, a great enemy and fierce opponent of the Church, into His humble and willing servant. It was nothing but God's sovereign grace that arrested Saul's heart and transformed him into God's greatest evangelist!

God didn't stop with Paul's conversion. His plan was so much bigger. He then used Peter to turn the beliefs of the Jewish Christian Church upside down — to ensure the Church knew the gospel, the good news of Jesus, was not just for the Jews but that Jesus came to seek and save all of God's people, Jews and gentiles alike. Paul took up the cross and carried it for Jesus into all the world, just as Jesus commanded.

The book of Acts created a blueprint for sharing the gospel. It set forth proofs about Jesus, and about our faith, that equip and embolden us to share the gospel more confidently and effectively. In these chapters, we experience the incredible working power of the Holy Spirit through fasting, prayer, baptism, miracles and faith.

And, you want to hear some great news? The presence and power of the Holy Spirit has not changed. He is at work in us, and in our midst, still today.

The call to Stephen, Phillip, Paul and Peter is still our call today: to pray, look and seek out every opportunity to share the hope we have found, no matter where or to whom God calls us. To break out of our routines and comfort zones. To overcome our fears. To invest our hearts. To be the vessel to bring God's created ones closer to His heart, His Word and the miracle-working, transforming power of His Holy Spirit.

Pray and ask God where He is calling you. To whom is He calling you to lead closer to Jesus. Remember, God's methodology hasn't changed. God continues His mission of sending, pursuing, seeking and saving today. God invites us, His beloved sons and daughters, to join Him on this mission. Won't you join Him?

# Pray
# this
# prayer
# with
# me.

# Heavenly Father, I want to share my faith.

Share what it means to live in the assurance of Your love and in the power of Your Holy Spirit. Teach me how to do it. Give me the confidence I need to take that first step. You are the Light of the World. Let Your Light shine brightly in and through me.

When I feel unworthy, anxious and afraid to step out in faith, remind me of who You are and who I am in You. Remind me that You are with me and You are enough. You are strong and courageous. You are my Strength and my Shield.

Lead me where You want me to go. Show me who You want me to speak to. When I'm with them, empower me with boldness. Fill my mouth with Your words. Anoint me with Your power. Give me Christ-like confidence and assurance.

Never let me forget that I am Your called one. Saved and redeemed so that I can tell my story and draw others into Your beautiful family, God.

I boldly declare this day that I am a child of God! Fear and intimidation will not stop me from sharing the good news of Jesus. Greater is the One who lives in me than the one who lives in the world. Thank You that no weapon formed against me will prosper as I go forth in faith doing Your Kingdom work. Thank You that, just as You were with Abraham, Isaac, Jacob, Joseph, Esther, Ruth, Daniel, Stephen, Paul and Jesus, You are with me wherever I go.

I am Your vessel, Lord, Your instrument. Use me. Empower me. Speak through me. Take the seeds I scatter and bless them abundantly so they bear fruit for Your Kingdom, now and for all eternity. I ask this in the name of the One who crushed the serpent's head, who is the Alpha and the Omega, my Savior and Redeemer, Jesus. Amen.

# longing for ———————— week eight
*week eight*

# Christ's return

# It's hard to believe we've reached our final week together.

Throughout our study, it seems clear that we long for what we love. I've personally experienced this with my kids. Something stirs in my heart when I leave for work and my boys run out the door chasing me, begging me to stay home. I respond, "Boys, dad's going to be home soon. I have to go to work." I close the door, and I can feel all six brown eyes staring into my back. The moment I left, the longing began because they love their dad. I'm not even sure how to describe how it feels when I come home and the boys run to me, hug and kiss me and shower their love on me. Why? Because from the moment I drove away, they were left longing for daddy to come home, and my return satisfied a longing that FaceTime chats, pictures, or a phone call just couldn't fill. They needed to feel the embrace of my arms and the warmth of my presence.

Since Genesis 3, we too have felt the absence of our Father's presence. Every step of the tremendous journey God's people found themselves on, they were waiting and anticipating a promise from God. They went through a wilderness experience longing for rescue, and they experienced a partial rescue and restoration, but they never truly experienced the fulfillment they so desperately desired. Why? Because while God graciously provided His partial presence for His people — the pillar of fire and cloud, the tabernacle, the temple — it was not the same as what Adam and Eve experienced in the Garden of Eden, walking and talking with God in the fullness of His presence.

Today, we may be tempted to say we haven't experienced exile or the wilderness, but if we pause and consider the journey of our lives, I think we can all admit to seasons when we've felt that way:

**The loss a family member**

**Deep hurt in our family or marriage**

**Uncertainty about our job**

**Hurt or pain due to illness or injury**

**Harsh words said to us that left us deeply hurt on the inside**

God designed us with a longing to have these pains met with something that would bring peace and healing. But, as we've studied, we often try to fill these longings with lesser loves. There truly is only one love that can sustain us and bring true healing and deep and abiding peace. That one love is the Love of God.

So, today, in the midst of our pain, let's praise God for His love and for the tremendous gift of His Holy Spirit who indwells His children and provides us with help, comfort, strength and courage to endure every crisis we face. Jesus, as He left the disciples said, *"It is not for you to know times or seasons that the Father has fixed by his own authority. But you will receive power when the Holy Spirit has come upon you, and you will be my witnesses in Jerusalem and in all Judea and Samaria, and to the end of the earth"* (Acts 1:7-8).

Not long after Jesus spoke those words, He ascended into heaven, and the angels spoke some of the most hope-filled words we have in Scripture to His disciples, *"Men of Galilee, why do you stand looking into heaven? This Jesus, who was taken up from you into heaven, will come in the same way as you saw him go into heaven"* (Acts 1:11).

We learn two important truths from this passage:

1.  Jesus left us with the Holy Spirit as a deposit and empowerment for His people to do and accomplish the will of the Father: to go and make disciples of all nations. In John 14-16, Jesus speaks of the coming Spirit and refers to the Spirit as the *Helper*. This comes from the Greek word *Paraclete* which means one who helps by consoling, encouraging or mediating on behalf of someone. [10]

2.  Jesus will in fact come back the same way He left. We live today in the "in-between" of the promise of Christ's return and the fulfilment of that promise with a clear picture and vision of hope that we can be confident in.

So, while we wait for the final return and rescue of Jesus, we live filled with hope and courage, empowered by the Spirit!

You and I have the hope of a future where we will enjoy the fullness of the presence of the Father, walking in the Garden City of Eden once again, hand-in-hand with the Creator God, our Heavenly Father. All of our longings will be finally and fully be satisfied as we enter and embrace the Father.

# Let's read, meditate on and long for this reality that is promised to all those who place their faith and hope in Christ:

*Then I saw a new heaven and a new earth, for the first heaven and the first earth had passed away, and the sea was no more. And I saw the holy city, new Jerusalem, coming down out of heaven from God, prepared as a bride adorned for her husband. And I heard a loud voice from the throne saying, "Behold, the dwelling place of God is with man. He will dwell with them, and they will be his people, and God himself will be with them as their God. He will wipe away every tear from their eyes, and death shall be no more, neither shall there be mourning, nor crying, nor pain anymore, for the former things have passed away." And he who was seated on the throne said, "Behold, I am making all things new." Also he said, "Write this down, for these words are trustworthy and true." And he said to me, "It is done! I am the Alpha and the Omega, the beginning and the end. To the thirsty I will give from the spring of the water of life without payment. The one who conquers will have this heritage, and I will be his God and he will be my son."* (Revelation 21:1-7).

Peter defended the gentiles
against the Judaizers at
the Jerusalem Council.
ACTS 15

Lydia believed
in the Lord
at Philippi
of Macedonia.

ACTS 16:11-15

God began inspiring
the the New Testament
writings of the Bible.
GALATIANS 6:11

Imprisoned
for healing,
Paul and Silas
were miraculously
set free and
their jailer
believed in God.

ACTS 16:16-40

Paul, Silas and Timothy
set out on their second
missionary journey.
ACTS 15:36;
SEE IN GENERAL
ACTS 15-18

**In Thessalonica, Paul and Silas were persecuted for** *"saying that there is another king, Jesus."*

ACTS 17:7

Paul preached to the men of Athens and some believed while others mocked.
ACTS 17:22-34

The biblical letters of 1 and 2 Thessalonians were written.

In Berea, they received the Word of God with all eagerness.
ACTS 17:10-15

**Paul reasoned in the synagogues of Corinth for many days before returning to the home base of Antioch of Syria.**

ACTS 18:1-21

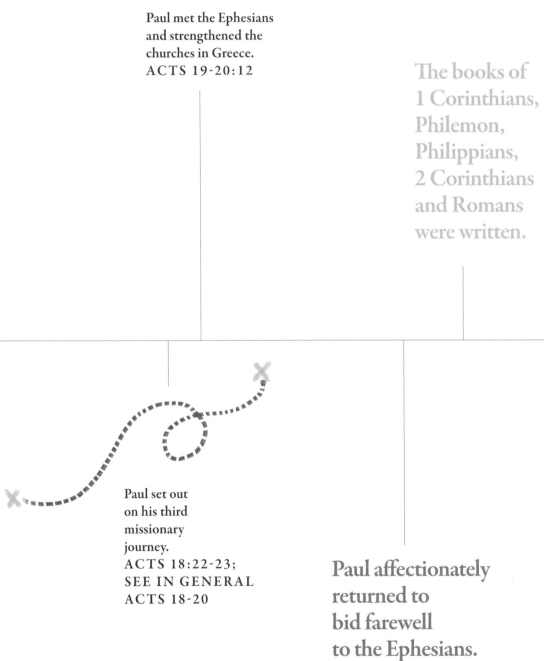

Paul met the Ephesians
and strengthened the
churches in Greece.
ACTS 19-20:12

The books of
1 Corinthians,
Philemon,
Philippians,
2 Corinthians
and Romans
were written.

Paul set out
on his third
missionary
journey.
ACTS 18:22-23;
SEE IN GENERAL
ACTS 18-20

Paul affectionately
returned to
bid farewell
to the Ephesians.
ACTS 20:13-38

# Paul ministered to the Roman government and the people of Rome.

ACTS 28:30-31;

SEE IN GENERAL

ACTS 25-28

Paul was sent to Rome by his appeal to Caesar and was shipwrecked on the way.
ACTS 27:1-28:16

After a riot in Jerusalem caused by his presence, Paul stood before both the Sanhedrin (the Jewish high council) and Felix (the governor) to defend himself.
ACTS 21-24

Paul defended the gospel before Festus and Agrippa.
ACTS 24:1-26:32

Paul made it to Rome and ministered there for at least two years.
ACTS 28:17-22

Jesus addresses His
Church as Lord.
**REVELATION 1-3**

Using seven seals,
seven trumpets and
seven bowls, Jesus said
He will both release
wrath as well as
gather a people
to Himself.
REVELATION 6-11

The books of Colossians,
Mark, James, 1 Peter, Acts,
Hebrews, Ephesians, Matthew,
Luke, John and the epistles
of John were written.

Jesus
disclosed
to John
that
He will
return
in glory
and final
victory.

**REVELATION 1:1-2**

Jesus said that the
Lamb of God is
worshipped in heaven.
**REVELATION 4-5**

**Evil
will be
finally
judged.**

REVELATION 17-20

The books of
1 and 2 Timothy,
2 Peter and Jude
were written.

**There will be a
new heaven and earth
and the tree of
life will be restored.**

REVELATION 21-22

**God opposes the
ancient serpent,
the devil.
REVELATION 12-15**

# The New Testament

God inspired the New Testament writings of the Bible.

---

*"See with what large letters I am writing to you with my own hand."*

GALATIANS 6:11

These past seven weeks, we've focused on 16 of the 66 books of the Bible. How I wish we could have covered every book, but that's nearly impossible in 40 days. So, today, we pause to celebrate the New Testament writing that's the first of Paul's many letters, his letter to the Galatian Church.

Let's jump to the last chapter of this letter for a moment. I'm touched by Paul's closing words, *"See with what large letters I am writing to you with my own hand"* (Galatians 6:11). By drawing attention to his handwriting, Paul reminds us in this digitalized world that the pages of Scripture were not typed or printed by a machine; they were handwritten.

01 | Do you often contemplate that the Bible began in handwritten form, or is this a fresh reminder? What thoughts do you have about this?

We find many theories as to why Paul drew attention to the fact that he personally wrote this letter to the church in Galatia. In Paul's time, authors often dictated writings of this length to an amanuensis, one who writes down the words for the author. We know, in fact, Paul used an amanuensis to write the book of Romans. (Romans 16:22) So, perhaps "large" referred to the letter's length.

But, considering the Greek word Paul used for the word "large," he was probably referring to the size of the actual letters. Some speculate Paul needed to write with large letters because of an eye problem that may have begun with his conversion and continued to plague him. (Acts 9:18; 2 Corinthians 12:7-10; Galatians 4:15). Others say Paul may have enlarged the letters for emphasis, much like we use all caps in an email or text.

Whatever the case, Paul's emphasis on writing the letter personally authenticated the letter and underscored the importance of his message.

*02* | **When was the last time you hand-wrote a letter or note to someone?**

Additionally, since we believe the Bible is the inspired Word of God, meaning God the Spirit led and guided every word each author wrote, Galatians is also God's handwritten letter from His heart to ours.

Also, let's not forget, God authored the very first words of Scripture ever written in Deuteronomy 10 when He etched the 10 Commandments into stone on top of Mt. Sinai. (Exodus 34:1-2; Deuteronomy 10:1-2) And, God continued to write His story, with great care and intention, through men like Moses, the prophets, the disciples and so many others.

Don't miss this powerful truth. God not only used His Spirit to inspire the writings, God the Spirit sits in the pages of Scripture, waiting for us to open it so He can meet us there and minister to us and speak to us. When we open God's Word, we are literally meeting with God. His presence is there with us. Teaching, reminding, convicting, encouraging, correcting and blessing.

Take a few minutes to read the following passages. Journal what you learn about God, Jesus, the Holy Spirit and the Word as you read each one.

**03**

*"In the beginning was the Word and the Word was with God and the Word was God"* (John 1:1).

*"And the Word became flesh and dwelt among us, and we have seen his glory, glory as of the only Son from the Father, full of grace and truth"* (John 1:14).

*"All Scripture is breathed out by God and profitable for teaching, for reproof, for correction, and for training in righteousness"* (2 Timothy 3:16).

*"... the name by which he is called is The Word of God"* (Revelation 19:13).

**04** Has your view of Scripture changed during this study? If so, describe how. If not, reflect on how your understanding has remained the same.

# The Second Missionary Journey

Paul, Silas and Timothy set out on their second missionary journey.

---

*"And after some days Paul said to Barnabas, "Let us return and visit the brothers*
*in every city where we proclaimed the word of the Lord, and see how they are."*

ACTS 15:36

Our verse for today marks the beginning of Paul's second missionary journey. Paul and Barnabas revisited every city from their first missionary journey and added Macedonia and Achaia (modern-day Greece) during their second journey, though not always together.

Their second journey didn't start well due to a disagreement between Paul and Barnabas. In fact, Paul refused to go with Barnabas if John Mark (Barnabas' cousin) accompanied them because John Mark, for unknown reasons, abruptly left Paul and Barnabas during their first missionary journey. (Acts 13:13) Perhaps Paul held this against John Mark. So, Barnabas took John Mark (Colossians 4:10) and sailed to Cyprus. Time seemed to heal their relationship. John Mark eventually penned the gospel of Mark, and Paul spoke kindly of Mark again as one *"profitable to him for the ministry"* (2 Timothy 4:11).

| | |
|---|---|
| *01* | Have you ever had a sharp disagreement with another Christian? Did you have to go separate ways? Were you able to maintain a friendship as Paul and Mark did? |

One of the most famous and remarkable events during Paul's second missionary journey was his speech to the people of Athens. Paul's teaching in Athens gained much attention, so the Athenians invited him to speak at a special place called the Areopagus. This area had once been used as a forum for the rulers of Athens to hold trials, debate, and discuss important matters. In Paul's time, Areopagus was where Athenian leaders and thinkers met to discuss matters of great importance to them. [11]

What seemed to set Paul apart is how he connected with his audience *before* he shared the gospel. He seemed to compliment them for being devout. (Acts 17:22) He used their idols and monuments to unknown gods as an illustration to point to the one true God. (Acts 17:23) He quoted their poets like Aratus of Soli, to talk about how we are *all* God's offspring, part of God's creation, originating with Adam. (Acts 17:28) He spoke in such a way as to win over as many as possible.

**02** Read 1 Corinthians 9:19. How does this verse relate to how Paul conducted himself? How have you been able to apply this to your conversations with those outside of the Church?

Paul's methodology sets a great example for us because Paul related and connected with those listening without ever altering or backing down from the unique message of the gospel. Paul unashamedly walked into Athens, with all of its deities and competing religious allegiances and boldly preached Truth. As those present listened to Paul's words, he received a mixed response. Mostly because the idea of a single supreme being who stood over the world and created all that exists was totally foreign to them. [12] Some believed his teaching, others considered it ridiculous, and still others believed divinity existed in heaven, but they also found divinity within themselves. Paul's message potentially threatened their way of life — if in fact it meant that they had to stop worshiping other so-called gods.

The point that finally divided the crowd in irreparable ways was Paul's teaching that God sent His Son Jesus to *"judge the world in righteousness"* and proved this by *"raising him from the dead"* (Acts 17:31). Many listeners considered Paul's words foolishness. That opinion has not changed today. Many today discount the gospel. Yet, it's the message God has chosen to be the very power of God for those who are being saved. (1 Corinthians 1:18)

**03** As you tailor the way you conduct your life to win as many as possible, are you still able to proclaim the full message of the gospel, knowing you may come up against opposition? Why, or why not?

# The Third Missionary Journey

Paul set out on his third missionary journey.

---

*"When he had landed at Caesarea, he went up and greeted the church, and then went down to Antioch. After spending some time there, he departed and went from one place to the next through the region of Galatia and Phrygia, strengthening all the disciples."*

ACTS 18:22-23

## Let's recall what we've studied so far regarding Paul's journeys:

1. During Paul's **first missionary journey,** he traveled through the regions of Galatia and was beaten with stones by Jews in Lystra after the people there called Paul and Barnabas gods.

2. During Paul's **second missionary journey,** Paul revisited the cities they had been to and ventured even further to Macedonia and Achaia (modern-day Greece), where he spoke to the Athenians in the Areopagus.

3. During Paul's **third missionary journey,** our topic of study today, Paul revisited the previous cities, focusing again on Asia Minor (modern-day Turkey) and one of its greatest cities, Ephesus, where he spent three years.

*01* | **Let's pause a moment and consider the miles Paul traveled, often on foot, risking his life, to tell the world his good news. What does this say about how much Paul believed the things he was saying? How does Paul's passion and commitment affect you and how you approach your journeys and conversations with others about the good news?**

The book of Acts records many events from Paul's third missionary journey, which spans Acts 18-22. Since we can't study them all, we'll highlight one major event: the Riot at Ephesus.

On previous journeys, Paul experienced his greatest opposition from the Jews. On his third journey, it was not the Jews, but the gentiles who opposed him most. The pagan culture awakened to the threat Paul's teachings posed to their economy. A silversmith named Demetrius, who created and sold silver shrines of the goddess Artemis, correctly assessed the impact Paul's words, *"gods made with hands are not gods"* (Acts 19:26), could have on his business and that of many other craftsmen and the economy.

02 | Most people today don't create replicas of Greek gods to worship, but what are some things we create or worship that we may treasure more than God? Has following Jesus ever made you nervous for losing those things?

Though Demetrius' concern was valid, he used that concern to play upon the people's emotions by invoking fear: Fear that they would lose their livelihood. Fear that Artemis would lose position and power. Demetrius' words enraged the people, creating a mob mentality and great confusion that led to the crowd dragging some of Paul's companions through the streets.

Finally, the town clerk quieted the crowd, warning them if they did not cease their behavior, they would be charged with rioting. He then released Paul and his companions.

03 | Read Matthew 16:24-26. In your own words, describe what the cost associated with following Jesus might look like today.

04 | Now read Matthew 6:33. How does this verse encourage us to be devoted to Jesus at all costs?

# Rome

### Paul ministered to the Roman government and people of Rome.

---

*"He lived there two whole years at his own expense, and welcomed all who came to him, proclaiming the kingdom of God and teaching about the Lord Jesus Christ with all boldness and without hindrance."*

ACTS 28:30-31

Today, chronologically speaking, we read the Bible's last words about Paul. We find ourselves at the end of what some have called Paul's fourth missionary journey, a journey very different from the first three.

In one sense, it was always Paul's intent to go to Rome. (Acts 19:21) But why and how he got to Rome was not his choice. Rather, it came about because the Jews incited a riot against him upon his return to Jerusalem. That riot ended with Paul's arrest and appearance before the Sanhedrin (the Jewish high council) and Felix (a Roman governor) to defend himself for preaching the gospel. (Acts 21-24)

Paul then defended the gospel before two other Roman officials, Festus and Agrippa. Agrippa was the Roman king of Judea at the time. (Acts 24:1-26:32) Finally, based on his Roman citizenship, Paul appealed to the Roman Emperor, Caesar, hoping for a more fair trial. This series of events is what led Paul to Rome. While on the way to Rome, his ship was caught up in a storm and shipwrecked for a time. (Acts 27:1-28:16) Eventually, Paul arrived in Rome and ministered there for at least two years. (Acts 28:17-22)

*01* | Can you imagine the time and effort expended by Paul just to share the Bible with people? Recount some risks you have taken to share the good news of Jesus. If you haven't yet, write down some ways you might begin to do this.

Luke leaves us in suspense about the resolution of Paul's appeal and end of Paul's life. Luke may have left this information out because it was common knowledge, or he didn't want to upset the official to whom he was writing. Whatever the reason, Paul's life ended tragically. According to ancient theologians and historians, Paul was beheaded in Rome under the orders of Nero. [13]

What I find fascinating and encouraging is that though we observe much opposition against the Christian message throughout Acts, we rarely see that opposition succeed. Not one leader found Paul worthy of indictment, and we find no actual record of Paul being found guilty of a crime. [14]

Though not indictment-worthy, the gospel was offensive then and still is today, because without context, it implies people are needy and weak, in need of saving from sin and sin's eternal consequences and judgment. The gospel goes further to say until God opens the eyes of a person's heart, calls them out of sin and darkness and into the light of His love and forgiveness through Jesus, they are condemned.

Yes, it's hard. Paul knew it was hard. But Paul knew he was sharing more than a religion. He was offering a powerful, life-transforming message he himself had experienced: new life and good news that offered the hope of forgiveness, redemption, resurrection and eternal life. Paul spent the last half of his life preaching this news and did it *at his own expense.* He lost his life for the sake of saving others.

Friends, we carry that same message in our hearts. We have that hope to give. We have that same call placed upon our lives to go out into our corner of the world to share the hope we've found in Jesus. And, yes, it won't always be easy. We need to settle in our hearts today that we are willing to be criticized, rejected, even persecuted, to share the good news ... the forgiveness ... the hope ... the peace ... the joy ... the love ... we've found. It's the best news in all the world! And, we do this all for Jesus

Paul did not do what he did for worldly gain. He didn't teach and preach to earn favor with God. In fact, Paul sacrificed much.

*02* | **What are some of the earthly things Paul may have given up through these journeys? Read Philippians 3:8-9. What does he think of the things he gave up?**

Some may argue Paul tried to store up treasure in heaven, but we know his treasure was Jesus because that is who had his heart. (Matthew 6:21) Paul said he suffered, *"in order that I may gain Christ"* (Philippians 3:8).

Paul encourages us to run in such a way as to receive the imperishable prize. (1 Corinthians 9:25) What he refers to here is running the race of life. To train and live disciplined lives that bring glory and honor to Christ. We run to receive a prize, a crown. But it is a *"crown of life"* (James 1:12), a heavenly reward that will never pass away ... eternal life with Christ.

Our faith in the death and resurrection of Jesus *compels* us to suffer, even die, for Jesus if we have to. But, we can take great comfort knowing we have the promise of resurrection and eternal life with Him in the midst of, and on the other side of, suffering. (Philippians 3:11)

Biblical scholar Gordon Fee says, "Our lives must be cruciform if they are to count for anything at all; but that reminder is preceded by an equally important one—the power of Christ's resurrection both enables us to live as those marked by the cross and guarantees our final glory." [15]

| 03 | **Can you imagine any scenarios today, or in the future, where your faith in Christ might put your life at risk? Describe such a scenario and what you might do.** |

# The Return of Christ

Jesus disclosed to John that He will return in glory and final victory.

---

*"The revelation of Jesus Christ, which God gave him to show to his servants the things that must soon take place."*

REVELATION 1:1

I find Revelation fascinating. It's filled with rich imagery, prophetic language and incredible promises about heaven. Because John wrote Revelation, we sometimes forget this book is "the revelation of Jesus Christ" (Revelation 1:1). John writes only what Jesus inspired him to write through the Holy Spirit. In fact — don't miss this — Revelation contains the largest sections of Scripture quoting Jesus' words spoken after His resurrection! (see Revelation 2-3)

01 | **Does knowing the words in Revelation are Jesus' words cause you to want to study it more? What questions do you have about this book?**

Here are a few major takeaways from Revelation. It contains the prophetic words of Jesus (Revelation 1:3) *"to show to his servants [us] what must soon take place"* (Revelation 1:1). Throughout its pages, Jesus addresses His Church as Lord. (Revelation 1-3) We see Jesus worshiped in heaven. (Revelation 4-5) Using seven seals, seven trumpets and seven bowls, Jesus says He will both release judgment and gather people to Himself. (Revelation 6-11) Jesus judges, defeats and overcomes the ancient serpent, the devil, and all evil. (Revelation 12-20)

Now, let's summarize what we've learned:

We learned in Genesis 1-2 that God created a perfect paradise, filled it with perfect creatures, two in particular — Adam and Eve — made in His image, who lived in perfect harmony with Him.

We learned in Genesis 3 that humanity had a problem with sin that began with Adam and Eve and has continued throughout the rest of God's story.

We also learned in Genesis 3 that God prophesied a plan of salvation to defeat sin, and the death that accompanied it. He progressively revealed that plan of salvation throughout the rest of His story.

We learned through all four gospels that Jesus came into the world, suffered and died for our sins and redeemed us, thereby making a way for us to be in right relationship with Him once again.

In Revelation, we learned the rest of the story. God's final ending to sin ... the hope that Jesus will once and for all heal the pain, hurt, loss and wounds caused by sin. Jesus will usher in the new heaven and the new earth. He will re-create, in an even greater and more glorious way, the first heaven and the first earth in which we now live. God leaves us with powerful, hope-filled promises. There will be no more pain and sorrow. No more tears and sadness. No more mourning and no more death. The perfection in Eden will be forever restored.

**02** | **Friend, are you looking forward to this day with eagerness? Read Hebrews 9:28. Sometimes we're tempted to hold onto this life because of unmet dreams or unfinished goals. What are some ways you can foster an eagerness in your heart for the return of Christ?**

# This week, we close our study of the Bible in 40 days.

What a journey we've taken together. We've learned how God created us with *longings* that only find their satisfaction through knowing and loving Christ.

We began in the Old Testament. From the creation of Adam and Eve and their rebellion to Noah and the flood to the tower of Babel to God taking Abraham from a land of idolatry, we see God's grace toward a people who tried to find their **purpose** apart from Him.

From Abraham's grandchildren to their slavery in Egypt to their release from captivity under Moses' leadership and God's giving of the Ten Commandments, we see God continually granting **freedom** to a people who insisted on seeking it from anyone and anything but God.

From God's people victoriously entering the Promised Land to them begging for earthly kings who fell short of God's glory to the destruction of Jerusalem to being taken into exile to 400 years of silence, we see a people who continued to desire security yet looked for that **security** outside of God.

After Solomon reigned, it wasn't long before God's people were in need of **rescue** from their own folly. As the kingdoms divided, they were eventually exiled and began a period of waiting for God.

We then followed God's story into the New Testament. From Jesus coming to earth as a baby to His three years of powerful ministry amongst His people to His betrayal and crucifixion to His glorious resurrection and ascension into heaven to the sending of His Holy Spirit to indwell all believers, we see God's people experiencing **fulfillment** and **redemption** in God rather than the things of this world.

From the beginning of the church in Acts 1, to the persecution of believers for sharing the truth of the risen Christ, to Saul's life transformation on the road to Damascus, to Paul's four missionary journeys where he shared the gospel, we see God's people learning their **identity** is found not in who they are or what they do, but in Christ and Christ alone.

From the many Holy Spirit-inspired New Testament writings, including the letters of Paul, to the book of Revelation, we hear the good news that Jesus is coming back for His people! That deep and abiding relationship God created His people for, the one they, and we, have been longing for since the Garden of Eden ... Jesus' glorious and final **return** ... is coming soon!

Friend, I pray the weeks we've spent together studying God's Word have encouraged and inspired you to go even deeper in your faith journey with Him. Rejoice in what He's done and anticipate what comes next! Watch for His activity and join Him. Let your life be a testimony both now and for all eternity! God will bless and reward you and take you on the most amazing journeys!

# Heavenly Father, You are so good!

We pray for Your Kingdom to come soon on the earth just as it is in heaven. Help us all to be a part of that mission. Let us tell the world of this good news to our family, to our friends, and even to those who are not our friends, so that all may come to know You and find their satisfaction in knowing You. Help us all to pay our bills, to clothe and feed our families, and take care of those in need. Forgive us where we have done wrong as we forgive those who have wronged us. Lead us away from all evil in the coming days if possible, but we pray for Your will to be done, especially if it brings You glory. You have given us great joy and peace, Father. You satisfy every one of our longings. Help us to know that better and cherish You in greater ways each day. In Jesus' name, Amen.

*notes from your study*

1. Augustine of Hippo, "The Confessions of St. Augustin," in The Confessions and Letters of St. Augustin with a Sketch of His Life and Work, ed. Philip Schaff, trans. J. G. Pilkington, vol. 1, A Select Library of the Nicene and Post-Nicene Fathers of the Christian Church, First Series (Buffalo, NY: Christian Literature Company, 1886), 45.

2. Heinrich Schlier, "Ἐλεύθερος, Ἐλευθερόω, Ἐλευθερία, Ἀπελεύθερος," ed. Gerhard Kittel, Geoffrey W. Bromiley, and Gerhard Friedrich, Theological Dictionary of the New Testament (Grand Rapids, MI: Eerdmans, 1964–), 496.

3. James Swanson, Dictionary of Biblical Languages with Semantic Domains : Hebrew (Old Testament) (Oak Harbor: Logos Research Systems, Inc., 1997).

4. C. H. Spurgeon, "Assured Security in Christ," in The Metropolitan Tabernacle Pulpit Sermons, vol. 16 (London: Passmore & Alabaster, 1870), 10.

5. John Calvin and John Owen, Commentaries on the Catholic Epistles (Bellingham, WA: Logos Bible Software, 2010), 288–289.

6. Forgiving What You Can't Forget by Lysa TerKeurst. Copyright © 2020 by Lysa TerKeurst. Used by permission of Thomas Nelson. www.thomasnelson.com

7. Breneman, M. (1993). Ezra, Nehemiah, Esther (electronic ed., Vol. 10, p. 118). Nashville: Broadman & Holman Publishers.

8. https://enduringword.com/bible-commentary/matthew-5/

9. David G. Peterson, The Acts of the Apostles, The Pillar New Testament Commentary (Grand Rapids, MI; Nottingham, England: William B. Eerdmans Publishing Company, 2009), 136.

10. Johannes P. Louw and Eugene Albert Nida, Greek-English Lexicon of the New Testament: Based on Semantic Domains (New York: United Bible Societies, 1996), 141.

11. Martin, H. M., Jr. (1992). Areopagus (Place). In D. N. Freedman (Ed.), The Anchor Yale Bible Dictionary (Vol. 1, p. 371). New York: Doubleday.

12. Polhill, J. B. (1992). Acts (Vol. 26, p. 372). Nashville: Broadman & Holman Publishers

13. McDowell, Sean (2016). The Fate of the Apostles: Examining the Martyrdom Accounts of the Closest Followers of Jesus. Routledge. ISBN 978-1-317-03190-1.

14. Polhill, J. B. (1992). Acts (Vol. 26, p. 414). Nashville: Broadman & Holman Publishers.

15. Fee, G. D. (1999). Philippians (Vol. 11, p. 152). Westmont, IL: IVP Academic

16. Robertson, A. T. (2009). A Harmony of the Gospels (Mt 13:51–53). Bellingham, WA: Logos Bible Software.

17. Bergen, R. D. (1996). 1, 2 Samuel (Vol. 7, p. 336). Nashville: Broadman & Holman Publishers.

18. House, P. R. (1995). 1, 2 Kings (Vol. 8, p. 93). Nashville: Broadman & Holman Publishers.

19. Casket Empty Timelines, Dr. Carol Kaminsky, CasketEmpty Media, LLC. © 2008

20. Breneman, M. (1993). Ezra, Nehemiah, Esther (electronic ed., Vol. 10, p. 118). Nashville: Broadman & Holman Publishers.

21. Matthews, V. H., Chavalas, M. W., & Walton, J. H. (2000). The IVP Bible background commentary: Old Testament (electronic ed., Mal 3:1). Downers Grove, IL: InterVarsity Press.

22. Blaising, C. A. (1985). Malachi. In J. F. Walvoord & R. B. Zuck (Eds.), The Bible Knowledge Commentary: An Exposition of the Scriptures (Vol. 1, p. 1583). Wheaton, IL: Victor Books.

23. John, John's Letters, Revelation, Biblica, Zondervan 2009

24. Images for Holy of Holies adapted from Faithlife Study Bible Infographics. Allen C. Myers, The Eerdmans Bible Dictionary (Grand Rapids, MI: Eerdmans, 1987), 204.

25. Hubbard, Shiloh, Elliot Ritzema, Corbin Watkins, and Lazarus Wentz with Logos Bible Software and KarBel Media. Faithlife Study Bible Infographics. Bellingham, WA: Logos Bible Software, 2012.

# About Proverbs 31 Ministries

She is clothed with strength and dignity;
she can laugh at the days to come.

**PROVERBS 31:25**

Proverbs 31 Ministries is a nondenominational, nonprofit Christian ministry that seeks to lead women into a personal relationship with Christ. With Proverbs 31:10-31 as a guide, Proverbs 31 Ministries reaches women in the middle of their busy days through free devotions, podcast episodes, speaking events, conferences, resources, online Bible studies and training in the call to write, speak and lead others.

We are real women offering real-life solutions to those striving to maintain life's balance, in spite of today's hectic pace and cultural pull away from godly principles.

Wherever a woman may be on her spiritual journey, Proverbs 31 Ministries exists to be a trusted friend who understands the challenges she faces and walks by her side, encouraging her as she walks toward the heart of God.

Visit us online today at proverbs31.org!

Proverbs 31
MINISTRIES